ROBBIE WILLIAMS
ANGELS & DEMONS

ROBBIE WILLIAMS
ANGELS & DEMONS

Paul Scott

André Deutsch

First published in 2003 by
André Deutsch Ltd
An imprint of the
Carlton Publishing Group
20 Mortimer Street
London W1T 3JW

A catalogue record for this book is available from the British Library

ISBN 0 233 00013 5 - Hardback
ISBN 0 233 00046 1 - Paperback

The publishers would like to thank the following sources for their kind
permission to reproduce the pictures in this book:

Section One:
Page 1, 2: Copywrite Media; Page 3: PAGE ONE; Page 4 Top: Zena Mellor/Rex Features;
Bottom: Rex Features; Page 5 Top: Copywrite Media; Bottom: Richard Young/
Rex Features; Page 6 Top: Copywrite Media; Middle/Bottom: Chris Grieve/Mirrorpix;
Page 7 Top Dave Hogan/Rex Features; Middle: Photonews Service/Old Bailey/Topham;
Bottom: Richard Young/Rex Features; Page 8: Brian Rasic/Rex Features,
Mick Hutton/Redferns.

Section Two:
Page 1 Top: Dave Hogan; Middle: Ray Tang; Bottom: David Abiaw/Rex Features;
Page 2 Top: Richard Young; Bottom: Brian Rasic/Rex Features;
Page 3 Top: PressNet/Topham; Bottom: Noble/Turner/Rex Features;
Page 4 Top: UPPA/Topham; Middle/Bottom: Jm Entertainment/Redferns;
Page 5 Top: Crispin Rodwell/Rex Features; Bottom: PressNet/Topham;
Page 6 Top: David Johnstone/Rex Features; Bottom: Aslan/Rex Features;
Page 7: PR/All Action; Page 8: Brian Rasic/Rex Features.

Every effort has been made to acknowledge correctly and contact the
source and/or copyright holder of each picture, and Carlton Books Limited
apologies for any unintentional errors or ommissions which will be
corrected in future editions of this book.

Typeset by E-Type, Liverpool
Printed and bound in Great Britain
by Mackays

CONTENTS

Prologue: From Tunstall to Tinseltown   7

1   Rituals   13

2   'Fatsykins'   25

3   Kick It   37

4   Mad For It   59

5   Fall–Out   71

6   Freedom   87

7   Showbiz Samaritan   101

8   Saviours   111

9   Angels   129

10   Grace   141

11   World Domination   155

12   The Ego Has Landed   167

13   80,000 Reasons to be Miserable   177

14   Straight Talk   191

15   Clean   207

16   Swinging For The Lonely   219

17   Cupid Stunts   239

18   The £80 Million Year Off   251

19   Pop Idol   265

PROLOGUE
From Tunstall to Tinseltown

The EMI executive clasped a half-smoked cigar between clenched teeth, thrust a sixth glass of champagne into the hand of his grinning colleague and looked through bleary eyes at his mobile phone. With dogged determination he slowly tapped out the number then gave a lop-sided, knowing smile to his A&R chum as he waited to be connected. 'Yeah,' he barked into the phone, 'I want to put three thousand quid on Robbie Williams topping himself in the next six months.'

Twenty feet in front of the couple sat the record company's newest talent. A little over a year after leaving squeaky-clean boy band Take That, Williams was making up for lost time. A few minutes earlier at the music business party in London's Mayfair, fellow guests had stepped over the 23-year-old singer as he clung to the floor of the Gents toilets in a £2,000 Dolce and Gabbana suit. Now wide-eyed and wired, he sat pouring vodka down his throat. 'Yeah, right, yeah, OK,' said the EMI man. He put his phone back in the inside pocket of his jacket and grabbed back his drink.

'What?' said his cohort expectantly.

'Bastard won't take my money,' he replied.

On an early autumn day in October 2002, a dark Range Rover navigated the narrow streets of Notting Hill, west London. 'Shall we pick up a DVD, mate?' Robbie Williams asked the driver from the passenger seat. A hour earlier the singer, all tattooed arms and Motley Cru sleeveless T-shirt, had stood outside the offices of his managers and yelled lottery winner-style at the assembled TV crews and reporters: 'I'm rich beyond my wildest dreams.' EMI had beaten off bids from Sony, Universal and Richard Branson's V2 label to re-sign Europe's biggest star with an £80-million record deal, Britain's biggest ever. Since parting company with Take That Williams had sold 22 million records, won a record nine Brit awards as a solo artist and gone from being pop's biggest loser to reaching his unquestioned position as the most bankable star in the business. For the one-time 'fat dancer' and member of Britain's biggest-ever boy band, who had self-destructed in front of the world, his rise back to the top from bloated, druggie alcoholic was complete.

It had been Robbie Williams, pop star, whose seemingly off-the-cuff declaration of joy over the deal, would get him on to every television news bulletin that evening and on to the front page of nearly every newspaper the following morning. Now Robbie had been put away until the next time a camera crew was on hand or he stepped out on stage. In his place was his alter ego, Robert Peter Williams, son of Stoke-on-Trent and sometime resident of London and Beverly Hills, California. There would be no celebration party for him, just home, a film and a cup of tea. Robbie was an invention, the creation of Take That manager Nigel Martin-Smith, 12 years earlier in Manchester. Nobody who knows him well ever calls him Robbie – they call him Rob. In fact he hates the name. Robbie is an invention, a larger-than-life character, often funny, sometimes crude and controversial, who is turned on and off by Williams. Rob, on the other hand is often quiet, filled with self-doubt, and sometimes loathing. He is troubled by his success but, at the same time, haunted by the fear that it might vanish. Robbie lives on the drug of adulation, the screams of 100,000 fans in a stadium, who are there just to see him, the rush of a record going platinum again. Rob suffers from depression. For almost a year he has relied on the 'happy pill' Ritalin to help him cope with the illness he has fought along with alcoholism for years.

The conflict between the two faces of Williams has become evident to those around him. On the one hand, he is the strutting, consummate entertainer, with the sort of charisma that can hold any audience. On the other hand, he is an often shy man, racked with nerves about having to talk to strangers, who can go on stage in front of thousands of adoring females and describe the experience as making him feel 'sad'. But the combination of the two characters – the 'love me, fuck you' dichotomy – is magnetically appealing. With Williams the music is almost secondary. Sure, there are those who don't get it, but to most the little boy lost combined with the 'I don't give a shit' swagger is mesmerizing.

What do you buy the man who has everything? Just before midnight on Christmas Eve 2002, two paparazzi decided to call it a night. They dismantled the lenses and flash power packs from their cameras and prepared to take Beverly Glen towards Sunset Boulevard. They had been tipped off that Robbie and lover Rachel Hunter were going out to a party somewhere in the hills, but there had been no sign of the couple tonight. Turning their SUV around and away from the gated estate where the star now lives, one of the photographers made a call. 'Yeah, we know he's there, but we haven't had a sighting of him today … No, fuck you. We're not coming back tomorrow!'

Five-and-a-half thousand miles away in his sister's modest home in Newcastle-under-Lyme, Staffordshire, Rob was waking up. The bodyguards who shadow him virtually every minute of the day were, for once, absent. So too, was latest celebrity girlfriend Rachel Hunter, who, we were told, was inseparable from her singer boyfriend. Instead, Rob was with his family: older sister Sally and her partner Paul Symonds and their two-year-old son Freddie, his mum Jan and father Pete. Rob had sneaked into the house and succeeded in giving the Press the slip. It was the first time for many years that the whole family had been together on Christmas Day. Not only was it noteworthy for bringing Pete and Jan, separated some 25 years earlier, together for a rare meeting, but it also signalled for Rob the end of a painful two-year hiatus in the relationship with his father. Now the day would be spent in simple, non-rock star fashion, the whole family singing carols, wearing paper hats, watching repeats on television and exchanging presents. The best for Rob was a framed aerial shot of his beloved Port Vale football ground in Stoke, which was given to him by his dad and now graces a wall in his Californian mansion.

CHAPTER ONE
rituals

It's the sort of ritual armies of weekend dads can identify with. OK, maybe not all estranged fathers take their eight-year-old sons to the bookies every Saturday to put their pocket money on the ponies, but kids like routine, don't they? So it was with Pete Conway and his son Robert. Pete had changed his name from Williams when he gave up his job at English Electric in Kidsgrove, Staffordshire, to pursue his dream of making it in showbusiness. The dream had come at a price: Pete's marriage to Rob's mother Jan had not survived. He had always remained in contact with Rob, but working all over the country in cabaret meant he was away a lot. Saturdays, when he was back in Stoke, belonged to his son. The ritual began with a visit to the park to play football. Pete loves sport. He had been a good footballer in his day and played cricket for the county. His love of football – particularly his adored Port Vale – was in the genes. Young Robert already had a good left foot, and, like all true Port Vale followers, hated rival team Stoke City with a vengeance.

The post-lunch ritual went like this: off to the bookies

where Pete and Rob would pick their horses, father helping son to fill in the betting slip. Then back to Pete's house for an afternoon in front of BBC1's *Grandstand*, cheering on their respective nags. It's a memory Pete has always cherished. He wanted to involve his son in his life and let him share his interests. Recently, father and son were reminiscing about old times and Rob said to Pete: 'Dad, I hated those Saturday afternoons.'

Pete Conway is a great bloke, everyone loves Pete. He is famous in Stoke-on-Trent, and struts the streets of Hanley like he owns them. You can't miss him in his gold Mercedes with its recently acquired personalized numberplates, perma-tanned and smoking a cigarette. At his regular hangout, Bar La De Dah, he is greeted the way Frank Sinatra once was at the Polo Lounge of the Beverly Hills Hotel. People stop him in the street to say: 'Alright, Pete?', and streams of women – young and not-so-young – pop over to his table to say a quick hello. Pete's always ready with a gag or a one-liner, even for the middle-aged lady with permed hair who tells him her husband has just left her for another woman. Pete's celebrity in Stoke has very little to do with him being Robbie Williams' dad. He has almost always been famous here.

Pete Conway often jokes that if he had remained in his first chosen profession, as a policeman instead of showbusiness, Robbie Williams would be pounding the beat now in the Stoke suburb of Tunstall. It's not really a joke: he means it and who knows, he could be right. Watch Robbie Williams work an audience and you see Pete. Robbie's style is a peculiar vaudeville, a sort of old-fashioned cabaret dressed up for the new millennium. Its spirit is of a different era, its heritage that of the northern working men's clubs, the *Wheel Tappers and Shunters Social*, and the smoky variety shows, which have died a slow death over the past 20 years. Robbie has said that he goes on stage trying to be Iggy Pop and ends up as Norman Wisdom. Seated night after night watching his father, dinner-jacketed, dicky-bowed, and 80s permed, Rob was marinated in the showman arts: Pete controlling the audience, cracking jokes and crooning a few Sinatra and Dean Martin standards at places like Perran Sands Holiday Park in Cornwall, or Haven Holidays in Great Yarmouth; Pete at the bar afterwards getting slapped on the back, having drinks bought for him.

But when it came to variety Stoke was King. Jollee's nightclub was the country's biggest venue of its kind, and had been voted the best in Europe. In 1974, the year Rob was born, Pete was appearing in front of an audience of two thousand people every night alongside such stars of club land as Frankie Vaughan and The Barron Knights. The same year he had a resident slot at the huge Talk of the Midlands club in Derby. In 1973 Pete had become a local hero when he won television talent show *New Faces*. When, a year later, he appeared on the *New Faces* winners' final, Rob's birth was portentously announced on air. Pete came third, one place behind comedian Les Dennis.

Today Pete doesn't work that much, the majority of his gigs are after-dinner speeches or benefits or involve helping out old mates. Approaching his 60th birthday, he is winding down a bit and there just aren't the venues for an act of his kind any more. His material is strictly family stuff. He doesn't do rugby clubs or stag nights and isn't one of the new breed of comics who rely on using the f-word 200 times a night to have their audience wetting themselves. In 2002 he left his job at Thorsby Hall in Nottinghamshire, where he had been resident host and compère for two years. The converted stately home had been taken over by Warner Holidays to offer 'adult only' vacations. But we're not talking hedonism here, more Sanatogen-fuelled mini-breaks for couples of a certain age who want a bit of a knees-up, a silver-service meal, the songs of yesteryear and a few turns around the dance floor on the hip replacement. Pete was mine host, introducing the acts, cracking jokes and telling the revellers what they had just missed on *Coronation Street* while they tucked into a carvery dinner. The highlight of the year for the guests and, one suspects, the lowlight for the staff, begins in October with the Christmas celebrations. Suspending their disbelief, guests arrive on 'Christmas Eve', despite the fact the leaves are still on the trees. The next day is Christmas Day complete with presents, a visit from Santa Claus and turkey lunch. This is followed by New Year's Eve and New Year's Day. Although he could eat for free in all the restaurants of the hotel, Pete chose to spent his time in his tiny staff flat in the roof of the building or out in nearby Worksop. The problem at Thorsby was that he was living in a goldfish bowl and couldn't walk ten paces without being accosted by yet another guest saying they saw last night's show.

Pete was a war baby, born on Boxing Day 1943. He's not aware there was any previous showbiz blood in the Williams dynasty. There were a fair few miners, though, and Pete's dad Phil was a bricklayer. 'Back then,' says Pete today, 'if you said you wanted to go into entertainment, your dad would say,

"Great, son, now go and get a proper job".' In 1949 Pete was sent to Tunstall Roman Catholic Mixed School. Standing nervously at the roadside with his cousin Christine Challenor, another girl, two years older than him, took his hand and helped him across the road. She was Teresa Jeanette Farrell, but everyone called her Jan. 'She was a dark-haired colleen of Irish descent,' says Pete. Jan, the daughter of John Farrell and Janetta Durber, was from Tunstall, Stoke. Her father had been a soldier and was now a building foreman. But Pete never thought she would look twice at him. 'She was the school beauty and all the boys fancied her, but I was two years younger than her and didn't stand a chance,' he adds.

The story should have ended there. At the age of 12, relatives offered Pete's parents the chance to take their son to America. In 1956 he made the 17-hour flight to New York, via Shannon in Ireland and Newfoundland in Canada with his mother Betty. Pete was enrolled at Belville High School in Belville, Illinois. He stayed five months, by which time his parents had decided the family were better off together in Stoke. Pete and his mum returned on the *Queen Elizabeth* to England. 'We were unique in Tunstall,' says Pete. 'Nobody had ever been to America.'

When Pete left school in 1960 he joined the police cadets and a year later, on his 18th birthday, he got engaged to local beauty Barbara Eeley, whose parents were neighbours of Pete's mum. The couple married in 1964 at the Sacred Heart Church in Tunstall. However, the marriage lasted less than two years. Barbara found it difficult to adapt to life as a policeman's wife, and was aggrieved to find that every spare moment her new husband had was devoted to 'the swimming team'. She was later to discover that the 'swimming team' was an elaborate cover set up by Pete and his pals in the force so they could go out on the town in Manchester with a string of different women. By 1966 Pete was single again and living with his mum and dad when he met Jan for the second time. Life on the force was already cramping Pete's style: he preferred nightclubs to night shifts. He left the police force to get a better paid job with English Electric and spent nights in the cabaret venues of Stoke wishing he could get up on stage and entertain the punters himself. His dreams came true when his mate, the local comic Tony Braddock, emigrated to Australia. Pete stole his act.

Jan, like Pete, had experienced a failed marriage. The difference was that she came out of hers with a baby. Sally was 18 months old when she and Jan moved into a small house in Victoria Park Road, Tunstall, with Pete. He was in the process of turning professional, perfecting his act, learning the art of timing and handling the pissed-up punters. The couple married in Stoke Register Office in 1970 with five-year-old Sally acting as bridesmaid. But, though the couple were desperate for children, nothing happened immediately. When, eventually, Rob was born on February 13, 1974, at the North Staffordshire Maternity Hospital in Newcastle-under-Lyme, Pete was already a well-known figure on the club circuit. He had won *New Faces* and was due to appear at the Talk of the Midlands in Derby with Frank Ifield on the night Rob was born. After seeing his wife and new son in hospital, Pete was so emotional he was shaking like a leaf and in no state to drive from the hospital to the club. Some friends took him there for his show and on the way back in the early hours Pete remembered he had some flowers for Jan in the boot of his car. He went to the hospital, used his legendary charm on the nurse and sat holding baby Robert on Jan's bed at 3 a.m. 'I was so happy we'd had a boy,' says Pete. 'We had a daughter in Sally. I always treated her as my own and she had been brought up with me. Having a son as well was perfect.'

On the face of it things were going pretty well for Pete and his young family. The couple had a nice house, two cars and a lifestyle that they could not have afforded if Pete was working in one of the local trades. Instead, he travelled the length and breadth of Britain, working in clubs as far afield as Aberdeen and Cornwall, sometimes staying away for weeks on end. Pete, the showbiz trouper, liked the nomadic existence, but for Jan, stuck at home with two children, the situation was less than ideal. When baby Robert was four months old, Pete was offered a summer season in Jersey in the Channel Islands. It was decided that Jan and the children would go with him. They rented a cottage in St Peter's Bay and stayed for four months. Thrilled that the whole family was at last together, Jan hatched an idea. Pete could give up life on the road. They could take over a pub in Stoke, cash in on Pete's local celebrity status and spend all their time together. From that moment the marriage was doomed. 'Jan quickly got fed up with my lifestyle, travelling all the time, always away doing shows,' says Pete. 'We decided to do something together. I didn't really want to get the pub because I was having a good run as an entertainer, but I just went along with the plan. If I had been honest I would rather have stayed with what I was doing.' He didn't have time for second thoughts. Two weeks after writing to the brewery, he was being shown how to change a barrel. In truth, Pete admits the marriage was already under pressure. 'Our marriage was rocky then because I was never there and Jan resented it. It is a problem with relationships with entertainers, not just me,' he says.

So in 1975, Pete reluctantly became the landlord of the Red Lion, an ugly 1960s boozer owned by Bass Breweries in the pottery town of Burslem. Pete handled the day-to-day running of the pub, while Jan dealt with lunchtimes and the catering. Conway continued doing the odd local gig, but his dream of the big time was put on hold. The life of a publican did not suit him. Sure, Pete was completely at home having a laugh and joke with the punters in the town centre pub, swapping a bit of banter in between pulling pints, but the relentlessness of the trade wore him down. 'You couldn't get away from it,' says Pete. 'As soon as you opened your eyes in the morning you were at work.' With his family in the flat upstairs and tension rising between husband and wife, Pete increasingly took to staying in the bar drinking rather than going back up to the flat and domestic strife. Pete describes Jan as 'confident'. 'Whether that's bossy or not, I don't know,' he says. You suspect he does. As well as running the pub, Jan was chairwoman of the National Housewives Association. She kept a watch on commodities that affected housewives, and made sure local shops weren't putting their prices up. She had her own slot on local radio. By the time the marriage imploded Pete and Jan had hardly exchanged a word for a month.

Pete Conway walks away. When things get difficult he's gone. There are more than a few women in Stoke-on-Trent

who'll tell you the same thing. He can't handle the aggravation. Given the choice of toughing it out, working out your
problems or bailing with just the clothes on your back, Pete's
already heading for the nearest exit. He's not blind to this
fundamental human flaw. He understands and accepts it.
When your trademark is a gag, a laugh and a pathological
aversion to anything vaguely serious, problems, especially
those of the female variety, can get in the way. Pete's philosophy is simple: 'Life's too short to be unhappy'.

On Saturday May 21, 1977, Pete left the Red Lion, his
wife, Sally and Rob to go to the FA Cup Final at Wembley.
He didn't come back. He didn't plan it that way, it just sort
of happened. As he watched Manchester United beat
Liverpool, he realized he was having a good time. 'It wasn't
my plan when I went to London,' says Pete. 'It became my
plan when I was standing on the terraces at Wembley. It was
the first time I had been let loose without the responsibility
of opening hours, work and the pub. I suddenly hadn't got
that and with all the aggravation that was going on at the
time with my marriage, I thought, "I'm free! This is what
freedom's like" and I decided that I wasn't going back.'

Pete was due back in Stoke on the Sunday morning. He
didn't show up and he didn't contact Jan to tell her he had
left her. Instead he stayed for three months in London with
his mate Mick. 'Leaving Rob was a hellish big thing, but I
thought he would be better off in a happy atmosphere. And
at the time we did have a very unhappy environment. I
probably handled it very badly, but I wasn't abandoning
Rob. I was just very unhappy and wanted Rob to be in a
happy place,' says Pete today. The Red Lion, Burslem, had

been anything but happy. Pete, not one to confront problems, felt better off out of it. Rob was with his mum, he'd be OK, he thought, and Pete felt the bad atmosphere was rubbing off on his son. 'It was just that everything was wrong with everything at the time and I couldn't live my life any more that way,' he adds.

The next time Jan saw Pete was when she heard him sheepishly knocking on the window of the pub after closing time one night. 'I had to let her know I wasn't coming back … I wanted my clothes,' says Pete. Jan wouldn't let him in. 'She wouldn't let me have my clothes. I had to start all over again,' he adds. What about Rob? How did this all affect him? Initially, the three-and-a-half year old seemed unfazed. Pete was out of his son's life for three months. The next time they met, there would be no emotional reunion, no slow-motion Hollywood-style embrace. Says Pete: 'When I came back to see Rob I went into the room and I was so excited and nervous. I thought he would be the same.' Instead, Rob, intently watching *Batman*, managed a 'Hiya Dad' and carried on watching the show. 'I thought he would jump up and down,' says Pete. When *Batman* finished he wandered over and asked his dad, 'Where have you been? What have you been doing?' Pete says: 'He had readjusted to his new lifestyle and I felt it was for me to cope with it more than anything.' Pete reasons that, at the time, he felt it would be better for Rob if his father was not coming in and out of his life, leaving the child confused. 'I know now that was wrong,' he says. Unlike Rob, Sally was old enough to realize what was going on. She had become and remains Sally Williams, but she found the manner of Pete's departure unforgivable.

Pete rang up his old contacts and said: 'Hello, remember me?' But the chance of making the big time was gone. Kevin Kinsella, the Manchester-based record label boss, who was Robbie's first manager after he left Take That, has been in showbusiness for 30 years. His assessment of Conway is simple. 'Pete is a very talented guy,' says Kinsella. 'He could have been a very big star, but he pissed it up the wall with Jan in that pub.'

So began the rituals: Pete and Rob off to the park and the bookies on a Saturday; Rob, spending the summer season with his dad in a caravan at holiday camps in Perranporth or Cayton Bay, Scarborough.

There's a brutal honesty to be learnt on the couches of £400-a-hour shrinks. It's that 'confronting the issues mantra' dished out to those looking for reasons why. Hence Rob's admission to his dad that he didn't like those Saturday afternoons. It doesn't take Freud to work out why. A child with feelings of abandonment making do with a few hours with the father who left him and, all the time, craving his complete attention. The same boy, who twenty years later, in the song "My Culture", wrote bitterly of his father, 'I wish he would hold me a little more than he did.' Pete says: 'Rob said he felt that the horse racing was something I did and it took me away from him even though I tried to involve him. He wanted us to stay in the park playing football, just the two of us, but he never said a word.'

CHAPTER TWO
'fatsykins'

If you get on the wrong side of Robbie Williams you're likely to end up getting the poetry treatment. His teachers got it, ex-bandmates and even his dad. His song "My Culture" is a rapped tirade at virtually anyone who has crossed him down the years. He changes the words to fit his latest victim. His milkman probably gets a scrawled version stuck in the top of his empties if he is late with Rob's two pints of gold top. Like a latter-day Gordon Gekko for the emotionally needy, Rob's message seems to be: 'Hate is good'.

It's an emotion used to stunning effect in his work. For every "Angels" there's an "Ego a Go Go" or "By All Means Necessary", Dylan-like personal onslaughts settling old scores. In "Ego a Go Go", which is a withering attack on ex-Take That colleague Gary Barlow, Robbie spits: 'Ego a go go now you've gone solo. Living on a memory. Where've you been lately?' And in "By All Means Necessary" he rants, 'All that make-up that you wear can't hide the flaws. Your charity work is for your own cause.' The angry young man persona is not a front. There's always been a burning resentment in

Williams, an unbridled fury at what he saw as his father's abandonment of him, the teachers who wrote him off and failed to spot his dyslexia, the cruel kids who christened their chubby classmate 'Fatsykins'. "My Culture", the song Robbie recorded with One Giant Leap, started out life as one of Rob's early poems entitled "Hello Sir". It begins: 'Hello Sir, remember me. I am the man you thought I'd never be. The boy who you reduced to tears. The lad called 'thingy' for six whole years. Yeah that's right, my name's Bob. The one who landed the pop star's job'. By the time it ended up on record the lyric had become a poison-pen diatribe aimed at his then-estranged father.

Rob has always had something to prove, a smouldering desire to achieve, a giant two-fingered salute to all those who had him down as just another waste of space. The 'look at me' instinct kicked in at an early age. He always wanted people to be impressed by him, he demanded their attention, stockpiled the tricks, the gags, the funny voices and impressions in case they got bored. Barely out of nappies, he would do impersonations of Margaret Thatcher, Frank Spencer and Brian Clough for the drinkers at the Red Lion. His dad Pete says: 'We used to close the pub and have a few people to stay behind in the bar. Rob was supposed to be in bed, but he used to come to the top of the stairs. There was a light there and it was his spotlight, that was his stage. He used to entertain everyone.' Rob himself has said, 'I could dance before I could walk and, literally before I could talk, I could sing and I found if I did that people smiled and paid me attention.' A less impressive party piece was throwing things from the upstairs window of the pub, including his mum's underwear and even the £2,000 takings on one occasion. He won his first talent contest at the age of three at the Pontinental Hotel in Spain, strutting and preening as John Travolta singing "Summer Nights". At four, on holiday with Jan and Sally, he wandered off. Jan found him singing and dancing for fellow holidaymakers with a hat placed on the ground for tips.

When he was eight Rob went to Zimbabwe with Jan where they stayed at the exclusive Victoria Falls Hotel. One day in the lobby, Rob spotted a group of machine-gun toting security guards surrounding the country's future vice-president Joshua Nkomo. Bold as brass, Rob strolled up, eyed the politician and declared: 'Hello, I'm Robert Williams from England and I can do impressions of black men.' He then proceeded to do his impersonation of Lenny Henry. Nkomo burst out laughing at this kid who wasn't scared of the guns and the minders and the pair sat down for a chat. He signed an autograph for Rob, who would later tell Jan with delight, 'That's the President of Africa.' Back home, Jan arranged for her son to model children's wear for fashion and bridal shows.

Summers were spent with Pete in a knackered caravan at Perran Sands, Cornwall, or the east coast resort of Scarborough. During the school holidays, Rob lived with Pete, emptying the bucket collecting the rain that dripped through the hole in the caravan roof, spending time with the Blue Coats, and gate-crashing the shows of resident double act Trafford and Wayne, Rob following Bill Wayne round the stage impersonating Max Wall's walk. He watched his father's act every night, laughing at the jokes as though he had never heard them before. When father and son sat watching *New Faces* on TV, Pete would say to the contestants: 'Open your eyes, son – let 'em in.' Rob still repeats the mantra to himself even now when he's on stage. When he was ten Rob told Pete he wanted to be a Blue Coat. Pete wasn't keen on the idea. 'I told him he'd have to do his apprenticeship somewhere, work the clubs like I did,' he says.

At Dolly's Lane Infants School, then Mill Hill Primary in Tunstall, Rob learnt quickly how to win over his classmates, particularly the girls. He was chubby and other children teased him about his weight, but he soon discovered a joke or impression defused the ribbing and 'fatboy' jibes. When Jan took him to school for the first time there were no tears from Rob, unlike the other children. He sent her home so he could get on with playing with the other kids. His teacher, John Collis at Mill Hill, remembers Rob's instinctive love and talent for drama. He was 'a natural', he says. By the age of eight Rob had become a member of all five major operatic societies in Staffordshire. He also busied himself with dance lessons, including tap. When Rob told deputy headmaster John Thompson he was going to be famous, the teacher told him not to waste time on silly dreams. 'I bet I end up driving a fast car before you do,' was the youngster's instant reply.

He won his first professional acting part at the age of nine, taking the leading child's role in a production of *Hans Christian Andersen*, followed by the part of Jeremy in *Chitty Chitty Bang Bang* at the Theatre Royal, Hanley. A week before the show was due to start the part hadn't been filled. The local television station ran a story with the reporter wrapping up his piece with an appeal for 'a boy over 4 feet, 7 inches tall and slightly on the podgy side.' Pete took him to the audition and popped over the road for a pint. When he got back Rob already had the part and was busy doing a read-through with his adult co-stars. 'He nodded at me. He was very relaxed,' says Pete. Encouraged by Jan, Rob went on to play one of the children in *The King And I* and, by the age of eleven, already a veteran, he played the Fiddler in the Theatre Royal production of the musical *Fiddler on the Roof*. There were pupils who gave their talented classmate the predictable 'big head' treatment, but Rob was almost universally popular with the other kids, despite regular appearances in the local paper, the *Evening Sentinel*. His puppy fat came in handy again when, at 13, he landed the role of 'Fat Boy' in a stage production of Charles Dickens's *The Pickwick Papers*. As the cast took its bow at the final curtain call, Rob found himself stuck at the back on a rickety, raised platform with the other minor characters. He turned to fellow society member Berenice Harrison and told her: 'I don't know why I'm here. I should be in the centre of the front row.'

There are certain pivotal moments in life when you know things are meant to be, when everything just falls into place. Rob picked up his hat, pulled a black woolly scarf tight round his neck, opened his eyes wide and lengthened his stride. A split second later he was in the lights, marching on stage. It takes a few moments to refocus when the spotlight assaults the retina. Blinded for an instant, your primary sense at that moment is hearing. What he heard was an audible gasp from the crowd. Rob was fourteen

It's some revelation when you realize that just your presence can trigger unrestrained excitement in an audience of adults when, by day, you are still doing double geography. Rob in torn frock coat, half-mast trousers, top hat and scuffed shoes with non-matching laces, stole the show as the Artful Dodger in the North Staffordshire Amateur Operatic Society's production of *Oliver!*. But it would be that sound – the spontaneous, communal in-take of breath, that unspoken mark of respect and admiration – that would out-live in Rob's memory the reviews, the pat on the back from the director and the picture of him leaning on a lamppost in the local paper. He'd got the role when Jan heard an appeal on Radio Stoke for a local lad to play the part. Rob beat the 150 who auditioned to win the role. The other stuff had been good fun, he got a kick out of being on stage, mucking around behind the scenes with the other kids, getting dressed up, but this was different. At that moment he became aware of the power he could exert over those people sitting in the stalls and circle. It was that X-factor you've either got as a performer or you haven't. If you haven't got it there's no amount of practice, no number of leotard-wearing, leg-warmer-clad teachers who can give it you; there's no *Fame Academy* remedy. If you're not born with it you might as well give up and think about a career in dental hygiene. Rob had it in spades. Pete had spotted his son's talent. During one performance of *Oliver!* his son absent-mindedly picked up two oranges from a passing fruit seller and expertly juggled them one-handed as he sang "Consider Yourself". 'Flash git,' an impressed Pete muttered under his breath.

At St Margaret Ward High School, Rob established himself as the classroom joker along with his pals Lee Hancock, Peter O'Reilly and Richard Cook. Lessons were 'a bind'. Rob went to school to have a laugh. Never a bad lad, he was the cheeky kid who loved to take the mickey out of his classmates and teachers. But, he was rarely cruel. Everyone knew someone like Rob at school. Look at him in his school photograph, back row, third from the right, in dark blazer, white shirt and striped tie, grinning through a tight jaw. The cockiness is there, the head tilted, the expression slightly mocking. All around him are either shy smiles, eager to please the photographer, job interview smiles, or from others, the fixed stare of the police mug shot. Even from thirty feet away Rob stands out, one eyebrow arched, grinning slightly too broadly, teasing, a hint of attitude.

Rob was popular with girls, but was no heart-throb. Still chunky, he found his best policy was getting them to laugh. His first kiss at the age of ten had been with a girl a year older than him. He took her to the cinema to see *Three Men and a Baby*. But the evening ended in disaster. They missed the bus home and had to walk through a red light district where two men threatened to beat up Rob. His date had to ring her mum to come and rescue them.

Rob made do with practising French kissing technique in front of the mirror at home. At high school his first crush was on an older woman. Kelly Oaks was 15, three years older than the young Williams. They were both members of the same operatic society and Rob fell for her instantly. He bombarded her with chocolates, flowers and cassettes of her favourite band Madness. But Kelly, who is now married and living in Hertfordshire, was not interested. She enjoyed having a laugh with Rob during rehearsals, throwing yoghurts out the window and watching them narrowly miss passers-by, Rob making a nuisance of himself, winding up the producers and dance instructors. In the end though, what girl of 15 wants to date a 12-year-old? They are more interested in guys a couple of years older than themselves. So Rob was on a loser with Kelly. She says: 'Rob was great. He was a real joker, but he was too young. At that age three years is a big difference.'

Undeterred, Rob moved his attentions on to Michelle Goodhall, famed for having 'the best arse at St Margaret Ward'. Rob was not immune to her charms. 'He was obsessed with my bum,' says Michelle. 'He kept trying to touch it.' The couple held hands and kissed a few times, but showing early signs of his magpie instincts when it comes to women, Rob lost interest after a couple of weeks. The first woman to break his heart was a girl called Tanya, who let 14-year-old Rob put his hand down her knickers when he was staying with his dad at Cayton Sands campsite in Scarborough. Rob hadn't realized she was leaving the following day and was distraught when he went round to her caravan the next morning and found she had gone.

He would have to wait another year to lose his virginity. The lucky, or as it turned out not-so-lucky, lady was a red-headed Liverpudlian called Ann Marie Lawson whose parents, George and Kathleen Lawson, had moved their family from their home town to Stoke. Ann Marie was in Rob's year at school and, according to Rob, 'loved sex'. As soon as she arrived at St Margaret Ward she marched up to a quivering Rob to tell him she was determined to 'shag' him. Rob, secretly petrified of the tall, upfront Merseyside lass, gave her the macho 'your place or mine' treatment. Later, in front of all Rob's mates, she strode over and told him: 'Your place, Friday after school.' Rob played it cool, pretending he had done it dozens of times. But although he fancied her, the intimidating Ann Marie scared the life out of him. Terrified, Rob took her home, but his legendary ways with women were sadly still in the development stage. They started kissing, but Rob lost his nerve. He couldn't go through with it, it wasn't right and, anyway, he was petrified. It was only as he was asking her to leave that he realized the stick he would get from his mates on Monday morning. He took her upstairs.

Years later he would recall of his first sexual encounter: 'I took her up to my room and about two-and-a-half minutes later it was all over. It was a less than impressive performance, but I was thrilled and naturally told all my mates what a stud I'd been.'

Rob never got into trouble with the police, but he was no angel either. He and his friend Matthew had a phase of stealing car badges. One day Rob stole the badge from a brand new BMW outside a pub. But shame got the better of him and he went into the bar and confessed. The pair gave up their crime spree when his friend's mum found out.

Lessons at school only served to get in the way of having a laugh or playing football. Rob, whose concentration span could be measured in minutes rather than hours, couldn't scrape up the enthusiasm to be bothered. But what teachers failed to spot was the fact he was suffering from dyslexia. It might only have been a mild form of the condition, but it was enough to make reading and writing difficult for Rob. Consequently, most teachers never took the cheeky kid with the smirk too seriously.

Forget *Goodbye Mr Chips* and *The Dead Poets Society*, all that Robin Williams crap about inspiring children, opening them up to art, music, literature. No, the most successful teachers are the ones who so provoke, so wilfully underestimate and stifle their young charges that those kids spend the rest of their lives striving obsessively for success if only as a massive 'f—— you', a huge one-fingered salute to the short-sighted prat who wrote them off. In fairness, when Rob came to give vent to his invective in his poem "Hello Sir" he created an amalgam, a composite hate figure, to be reviled and despised, to get it from both barrels for all the slights and the put-downs he received from the teaching profession. But there always has to be a fall guy: step forward Steve Cartlidge, who actually only taught Rob for his last year at St Margaret Ward High School. His mistake was offering careers advice as well. In the poem, which originally appeared in the anthology *Oral: Poems, Sonnets, Lyrics and the Like*, Rob rages at the teacher who advised him to join the army, the 'plonker' with 'receding hair', 'fake sports car' and 'dodgy Farrah trousers'. Although Mr Cartlidge says he always wore smart suits to school, he accepts the poem was, in part at least, written about him. But he is unapologetic. 'I merely gave Robbie some sound career advice,' he says. 'I told him that entering showbusiness is all very well, but he should concentrate on getting qualifications and passing his exams. Nowadays, I use Robbie as an example to engender ambition in children I teach. I tell them that if their hearts are set on a particular career then they should go for it. And never mind the advice of a tired old English master.' Mr Cartlidge says he doesn't bear any grudge against Rob, but adds, perhaps somewhat churlishly: 'Robbie must be a late developer because the English he uses in his song lyrics is very impressive, well worth marks of grade C or above.'

Such was Rob's desire to prove his old teachers wrong, that when he found fame he would later return symbolically to his old school in a BMW and wearing a £4,000 suit. He pulled up at the gates, sounded the horn and shouted: 'Up yours'. His friend Anthony Robinson, who used to stand on the terraces at Vale Park with Rob, says Rob always wanted something more than most of his school friends could look forward to in Stoke. He would tell his friend: 'I'm better than this. I'm going to get out of this.' Says Anthony: 'He got a lot of his drive from his mother's side. She was very supportive of him. She would push him all the way.' Rob, says his friend, wanted everyone to like him. 'He wants you to look at him. He makes sure he is liked because he has a fear that you won't like him.' However, while still at St Margaret Ward, grade C or above was not on the agenda for Williams minor. In fact, it was fair to say that no one, including Rob himself, expected him to pass a single GCSE when he took his exams in June 1990. At the end-of-year disco, Rob took to the stage and sang "Every Time We Say Goodbye". The effect on his hormonal female classmates was prophetic. There was much weeping and swooning as Rob showed off his, hith-erto, at school at least, well-hidden singing voice. The reaction from the boys was also to set the tone for the next five years. They booed, jeered and generally took the piss.

Now it was time to think about earning some money. One of Sally's boyfriends found him a job selling double-glazing door-to-door. Rob lasted three months, but it was clear from the outset that a career in direct marketing was not for him. 'I used to tell people the windows were over-priced and leave,' he says. When his dad Pete asked him how his new career was going, Rob told him he was being 'told to 'eff off all over Staffordshire'.

But, for Rob, the job was only ever a way of earning a few quid in the holidays. The dream was still to make a career in showbiz. Jan had seen a newspaper ad seeking a fifth member of a band being put together by an impresario from Manchester whose name was Nigel Martin-Smith. The group would be called Kick It.

CHAPTER THREE
kick it

Given Rob's future battle with drink and drugs, it was either through good luck or good management that Kick It was dumped pretty quickly as the name for the new band. But Kick It was its name when Rob applied for the job his mum had seen advertised in *The Sun*. At that point the band was already in existence: singer Gary Barlow, dancers Jason Orange and Howard Donald and pretty boy Mark Owen had been assembled by Manchester model agency boss Nigel Martin-Smith. His idea was to create a British version of the phenomenally successful US boy band New Kids on the Block. They had five guys, so too, decided Martin-Smith, would Kick It.

Jan enlisted the help of Pete's pal Pat Brogan, a local boxing promoter, to give her advice on how to give Rob the best chance of winning the remaining fifth berth in the new group. Pat rang his friend Chris Fear at BBC Manchester and asked him if he could make the introduction to Martin-Smith. The following day, Jan typed out Rob's CV. It told Martin-Smith Rob had done work experience at Stoke commercial station Signal Radio where he had also done some voice-overs and had applied for a job in hospital radio. It also said that he had been writing his own rap and hip hop songs before signing off with the words, 'I have only one ambition, which is: TO BE FAMOUS.'

Jan got word from Manchester that Rob had got an audition for the band during the summer of 1990. The only problem was that Rob was in Wales staying with his dad at the Carmarthen Bay Caravan Park where Pete was entertaining the campers. Jan, in a state of excitement, began trying to get hold of Pete. He didn't have a phone in his van, so the reception staff were dispatched to track him down. Eventually he took Jan's call at the front desk and then began solving a problem of his own – where the hell was Rob? It was not unusual for Pete not to see Rob all day. He had the run of the site and with the amusement arcade, beach and a ready supply of girls to chase around, there was a lot to keep him occupied. But Pete promised Jan that he would get their son on a bus back to Stoke the same day and so he set off trying to track down his missing offspring. An all-points bulletin was put out in the camp and Rob was unearthed. But before sending him back to the Midlands, Pete corralled the campsite's official photographer to take Rob on to the beach and do his first photo shoot as a 'pop star'. The two black-and-white shots show Rob with quiffed hair and in one he is wearing trademark star shades. If anything can be said to mark the transition from Robert Pete Williams, Tunstall school-leaver and academic failure, to Robbie Williams, boy band pin-up, it's all there in those two images.

Pete, more excited than he cares to admit, got Rob's stuff

packed up and drove him to the bus station in nearby Carmarthen. But in his eagerness to get there on time, Pete forgot his car had no petrol. As they reached the top of a steep hill, the car's engine spluttered and died. Pete let it coast down the hill and pulled into a pub, coincidentally named the Red Lion. He threw himself at the mercy of the landlord and bummed the pair of them a lift to the bus station.

Nigel Martin-Smith's plan was simple. He wanted to put together a group of good-looking young lads, polished, marketed and shrink-wrapped and watch the money roll in. Right from the start, the band that within a few weeks would become Take That – the name was stolen from the words 'Take That and Party' on a Madonna poster – was about making as much money as possible in the shortest possible time. Rob went to the audition at Martin-Smith's Manchester offices with his mum. By the end of their meeting Martin-Smith knew Rob had to be in the band. 'His mum had obviously told him how to leave a room properly like they teach girls at charm school,' recalled Martin-Smith. 'There was just this glint in his eye as he looked at me and I thought, "You've got be in the band".' In a nearby club the five sang "Nothing Can Divide Us", some more passably than others, but Martin-Smith was satisfied the look was right. He took them to Boots for a cup of coffee to celebrate the band's birth. The manager, whose previous claim to fame was looking after a singing drag queen, told them that if they gave him five years he would make them all rich. But it would be at a cost. There would be strict rules – nothing would be allowed to damage the carefully planned image: no girlfriends, no drink, no cigarettes and no drugs. They would avoid the usual celebrity hangouts, keep a mystique about them. There would be no paparazzi photographs taken outside nightclubs such as Stringfellows or Browns of the boys with dubious blondes. They would stay in Manchester and keep their private lives out of the limelight. There would, Martin-Smith told them, '... be six of us in this band ... If we stick together, form a wall around ourselves and keep away from parties, the tabloid Press will have nothing to knock us with when we achieve fame,' he reasoned.

Gary Barlow would be the focal point of the band. He had a track record on the club circuit already and had written some classy pop songs. Howard and Jason were known as two of the best break-dancers in the northwest. They formed a duo called Street Beat and were spotted by Martin-Smith performing on Pete Waterman's late-night television show *The Hitman and Her*. Mark had a decent voice and could dance. He had met Gary a year before when he had been the tea boy at a studio in Manchester where the singer was recording. Mark began helping Gary to lug his gear around his gigs and they formed a band together called the Cutest Rush.

Rob was told he had got the job in the band the same day he received his exam results. He had failed the lot. He and a friend bought eight cans of Newcastle Brown Ale and downed them on the bowling green in Tunstall. Eventually, Rob had the courage to go home and tell his mum the bad news. 'Mum, I've got something to tell you,' he started meekly. 'Well, I've got something to tell you. You're in that band,' was Jan's reply. Rob ran upstairs, flung open his bedroom window and shouted to anyone who would listen: 'I'm going to be famous!' At 16, Rob was the youngest band member by almost two years. Yes, he could sing and dance a bit, but, to be honest, neither skill was much to write home about. Rob was primarily there to add a bit of personality – a cheeky attitude, a bit of an edge. It would seem a bit rich then that over the next five years it would be these very traits that would land him with so much flak from his manager.

Even before contracts with Martin-Smith were signed in September 1990, the strategy for the band was taking shape. One of the first things was to relieve Rob of his name. His new moniker, Robbie, said Martin-Smith, was more fun, more mischievous. Hardly anyone had ever called him Robbie before. Rob hated the name from day one. He would also have to lose weight, ruled Martin-Smith, and work hard on the dance routines that the others mastered way before him. The next step was to get the band's image right. The official line is that Nigel Martin-Smith took the five lads to London for a shopping trip. There, in Hyper Hyper in Kensington High Street, Jason spotted a leather jacket with tassels and the leather look was born. In reality Martin-Smith was already pitching the newly incarnated Take That at a gay audience. Later, Martin-Smith, who is himself gay, would claim his plan had been to create an ambiguity, to keep the audience guessing which side his boys batted for. If that was indeed the strategy, something had gone very wrong between the planning stage and the end result. When they did their first TV appearance, miming to a tape in a dance studio in Manchester on the local BBC evening news programme *Northwest Tonight* in October, there wasn't much ambiguity on show. In fact, they couldn't have looked more gay if the five of them had minced around Union Square in San Francisco, clutching *Abba* albums and whistling show tunes and shrieking, 'You bitch!' at each other. Gary, his blond hair spiked, went topless with a red handkerchief tied round his neck, skin-tight red satin three-quarter-length trousers, and a black leather belt. Mark looking like Central Casting's stock rent boy, was all peroxide and body piercing; Howard was dressed in tiny cut-off denim shorts and baggy T-shirt, and Rob wore a spray-on cycling top and shorts emblazoned with the Pepsi logo. The only thing missing from the image was a smattering of handle-bar moustaches and a couple of leather caps.

The image was blatantly homosexual: they were the embodiment of turbo-charged gay fetishism. The gay fan-base and pink pound were a major lure to Martin-Smith who understood that scene far better at that stage than he did teenyboppers. Anyone who saw them then would have been forgiven for thinking they were a gay band. The majority of their gigs were on the gay circuit. Take That's first concert was in front of 'ten people and a dog' at Flicks nightclub in Huddersfield. The band got £20, barely enough for Kentucky Fried Chicken. But their dance moves were already working well and Gary was displaying the skills as a singer and songwriter that would see him bank several million pounds in the next three years. Rob's voice was not of immediate importance to Martin-Smith, any bum notes could be ironed out in the recording studio and, anyway, the priority was the look and the stage show.

Rob was never given a singing lesson during his whole time with the band. A mini-tour of Scotland was arranged for April 1991 and Nigel set about plans to release the band's first single "Do What U Like", the video for which showed the lads rolling around in red jelly. The problem for Martin-Smith was that, despite relentless pitching to the majors, no record label had bitten. This left him with Plan B – to mortgage his house and put the record out on his own label Dance UK. The gamble worked. "Do What U Like" entered the UK chart at number 82, but it was enough to snare RCA who signed the band in September 1991. The five lads were flown to London to put pen to paper and were picked up in a limousine at the airport. They thought all their Christmases had come.

The band may have had a deal, but for Pete and Jan there was still the concern about just what sort of band Rob was involved with. Pete knew the business, he was more than aware that showbusiness was populated by homosexuals and wasn't overly concerned. Rob's grandmother Betty told Pete, 'I'd be more worried if he said he was becoming a priest.'

But it was Rob who came closest to writing himself out of the pages of musical history. Even after only a few months he was already regretting joining Take That. His relationship with Martin-Smith had become difficult very early on. Rob told Jan he was sick of being treated like an idiot by his older band mates and getting regular bollockings from Nigel Martin-Smith. He told his father: 'I'm only there to be a backing dancer for Gary Barlow. I've got my own ideas. I want to be at the front.' He said he was thinking about leaving and asked his dad about becoming a Blue Coat. Pete knew Rob was unhappy, but was quick to tell him that his unhappiness now would be nothing compared to his heartbreak if he walked out on Take That and they had a big hit. So, with more than a few misgivings, Rob bit the bullet and toughed it out. It would be two years of hard slog, failing to dent the singles charts and desperately trying to build up a fan base. A second single, "Promises", entered the chart at number 38. The boys were so excited they jumped up and down on Howard's bed at London's Regency Hotel so hard that they broke it. It was to be one of their few collective acts of rock'n'roll mayhem. The joy was short-lived. The following week the single dropped to number 40. Single number three, "Once You've Tasted Love", only reached a disappointing number 44. Meanwhile, the band would often find themselves performing four shows a day. They embarked on a school tour in conjunction with the Family Planning Association to promote safe sex. Often they could expect to do a show at a school in the morning, a matinee show, an under-18s club and an over-18s club all in the same day before getting back into Nigel's car and heading home or to a cheap hotel.

Yeah, sure, Gary was the grown-up, the assured lead singer and Mark the good-looking one, but it was Rob who was increasingly not only stealing the live show, but wresting it manfully from his all-singing, all-dancing colleagues. He can't help himself. Put Rob on a stage, be it Wembley Arena or the far end of the sports hall at a school in Worksop, and he's unstoppable. While the other four were ultra-professional and stuck closely to their dance routines with fixed smiles, Rob could never resist a few twists on the meticulously thought-out shows; gurning at the audience, the occasional Norman Wisdom-style fall or a bit of banter with the crowd. He was always at pains, either consciously or subconsciously to impose a bit of himself, a part of Rob from Stoke, on to the almost military precision of the proceedings. The scene-stealing came naturally. There was no conscious plan to grab the attention away from the others. It was just part of the package. But, undoubtedly, it riled his band mates and often Martin-Smith too.

The band's first real hit, "It Only Takes A Minute", was released in May 1992, entering the chart at number 16 and peaking at number seven, but even before this there were real tensions between the boys. Perhaps it's not that surprising. You can't take five kids and throw them together virtually 24 hours-a-day, in the car, on stage, eating together, sharing hotel rooms and expect there not to be problems. Rob was closest to Mark. Like him, Mark was a sensitive character who didn't relish confrontations. Gary was always going to be the one most likely to have a problem with the youngest, mouthiest member of That That. With good reason, Gary was entitled to think that this was his band. He wrote most of their songs, did almost all the lead vocals and was increasingly involved in shaping the way they sounded in the studio. You don't set your heart and soul on grabbing fame; you don't work like a dog in grotty clubs and disinfectant-reeking school gyms without that drive, that ego forcing you on. It's a prerequisite for success. How else would you take all the let-downs, the rejection, the fear of failure that goes with trying to crack it in showbusiness? Gary, like Rob, had been endowed with an ego that was larger than most. There was always that tension between them, Rob jealously eyeing Gary's position as head honcho, the frontman, the leader. Gary, who had dreamed of emulating his heroes Elton John and George Michael, covetously watching Rob's easy charm, his effortless charisma and presence. It was plain to those around the band, even at the outset, that the combination of the two personalities would be flammable. 'They were an accident waiting to happen,' says one who was there. 'Others could see it, but to start with neither Rob nor Gary saw the potential for the hostility that eventually came.' When Rob sang a tune he had written down the phone to Gary once, there was silence on the other end of the line. Eventually, Gary said, 'That's all right, that, lad.' He then turned to someone in the room with him and said, 'That Robbie's started writing stuff. It would be all right if we were in a rock'n'roll band.' Gary, who was so notoriously tight with his money that he actually liked his nickname of Ebenezer Barlow, took to charging Rob a pound every time he lent him his mobile phone.

When the band were being driven back to Manchester in the van after a gig, Rob would be dropped off at junction 16 of the M6 and his mum would drive over to pick him up from the roadside. The success of "It Only Takes a Minute" served to define the real audience for Take That – schoolgirls. The overtly gay image was dumped, although the tag and the gay fan base would endure. The boys finally knew they they'd made it when they went out to dinner at La Reserve restaurant in Fulham. The single had gone into the Top 20 and, as they sat eating, a group of girl fans assembled outside and broke into spontaneous sobs when they caught sight of their new heroes. The dreaded 'Thatter' was born. Their next single "I Found Heaven" saw the band shoot their first video. They had been told it would be on a beach. They envisaged Mauritius or Marbella, but got the Isle of Wight, dancing and singing for hours in the freezing sea. By the time "A Million Love Songs", a Gary-Barlow-penned weepie, got to number seven in September 1992, as many pre-pubescent girls were raiding W.H. Smith for a poster of the band and the Blu-Tack. The tight satin and leather was gone and in came the baggy uniform of the street – combat boots, sweaters and denim jackets.

A remake of Barry Manilow's "Could It Be Magic", on which Rob sang the lead vocal, and single number eight, "Why Can't I Wake Up With You", in February 1993, confirmed Take That as the biggest thing in British pop. Rob would wake up on a Sunday morning at his mum's house to find 300 girls outside and the police out in force to cordon off the road. What's the next most likely move for a band that have been making hit records for less than a year? Write your autobiography, of course. The idea was to give their fans – at £5.99 – an insight into the symbiosis at work in the band, the genesis of their musical style, oh and which girl they first kissed and what football team they supported. Like everything else about Take That, it would be a well-controlled exercise in maximum exposure and maximum profit. The boys could witter on about kissing Karen or Michelle when they were twelve. (Was it any surprise that Gary's first kiss with Melanie Garnet when he was eight turned into 'quite a steady relationship for four years'?) The problem, though, as usual, was Rob. From page 31 to page 36 of *Take That –*

Our Story, Rob had gone from saying he got 'eight or nine GCSEs at St Margaret Ward' and saying he was still registered in the sixth form there, to admitting that 'When I left school, I thought, right, I've got no qualifications'. If the book proved anything, though, it was that Rob, unlike the others, just couldn't do bullshit. 'I remember thinking what a weird bunch of lads they were,' he said about the first time he laid eyes on his fellow band members at his audition. And, when it came to the band's front man Gary, Rob was incapable of playing the PR game the way his Take That keepers would have liked. In the beginning, Rob revealed, he found Gary 'boring'. 'He was really hard to get to know and he wasn't letting anyone inside his head,' said Rob. A year after being let off the Take That leash, Rob would add new insight into his first impressions of Barlow at the Take That auditions. 'There was a guy, sat there. He's got his legs crossed and this bloody leather briefcase which had song sheets for crap cabaret songs in it,' he sniped.

In a three-month period between July and September 1993, the band recorded their first two number ones. First, "Pray" and then "Relight My Fire", a three-minute screech-athon featuring former *Eurovision Song Contest* entrant Lulu. The video, shot in London's Ministry of Sound, will long live in the memory as one of the more excruciating moments in recent pop history. A pre-botox Lulu having it large like an embarrassing mum, who insisted on coming to the school disco, promised to stay out of the way and ended up alone on the dance floor at the end of the night doing a Mick Jagger walk while everyone looked away. Rob was becoming increasingly embarrassed about Take That. The whole image was naff, not at all how he had planned it. The fame was one thing, but for half the country, Take That were only famous as a bunch of wankers wearing Converse trainers. He reverted to his tried and tested antidote to the mickey-taking he got at school and joined in the joke. 'What do you call a singer with five arseholes? – Lulu and Take That', he quipped.

In 1994, 16 singles into their career, the band were still surviving on the £150-a-week they were paid by their management. But they were now huge. Already being called the 'The Beatles of the 1990s', tours of virtually every European country were undertaken as well as Japan. Even in the States, *Rolling Stone* magazine called them 'the hottest teen idols in the world'. Back home, Jan's florist's shop, Bloomers in Tunstall, was the scene of daily vigils by hundreds of female fans. The crowds became so big she had no choice but to shut the business down because customers couldn't get inside. She also put her home in Greenbank Road, Tunstall, on the market and moved out after it became a shrine to fans who would take coach trips from Scotland or Devon to traipse up Jan's path and plead with her to let them see Robbie. Jan worried about the kids and was devastated when one girl arrived in a wheelchair, telling Jan she was terminally ill and wanted to meet Robbie before she died. Rob's grandmother Betty got into trouble with Nigel Martin-Smith for letting fans into her house for a chat and cup of tea. Betty, not one to be pushed around, told her grandson's boss to keep out of her business.

Rob, too, was getting fed up with the rules. There were regular 'Behaviour Meetings' at which it would be Rob who'd get the flak about not playing by the Take That code. Either Martin-Smith or the members of Take That themselves would call them. Rob could never recall a meeting being called to discuss any misbehaviour by the others. He christened the system of rules and strictures 'Take That Towers'. He was already testing the regulations, pushing the boundaries. Where once Rob would have apologized for being photographed out on his own or with a girl, he was now more likely to argue the toss, refusing to see anything wrong in his behaviour. On tour he had taken to flouting the rules. He openly bragged that, when the band was staying at the exclusive Loews Hotel in Monte Carlo, a girl he met in the bar pressed a piece of paper with her room number written on it into his hand. Later, a drunk Rob found the note while he was undressing for bed. He realized her room was just along the corridor, but knew he could not risk being caught by the ever-watchful Martin-Smith. Too drunk to realize the danger, he vaulted over several balconies high above the sea and knocked on the girl's window. It was only then he realised he was completely naked.

In 1994, a year before his Take That career imploded with his drunken antics as Oasis's uninvited backing singer at Glastonbury, Rob had gone to the music festival. Still too nervous of Martin-Smith to take him on with a public show of disobedience, instead he spent the whole time in M People's van getting drunk with Feargal Sharkey, terrified he would get spotted by photographers. Martin-Smith took to writing his difficult star letters telling him what was expected of him. Rob also accused him of writing to tell him he was out of the band if he didn't lose weight. Still the work was relentless. In September 1994 alone, Take That performed 22 arena gigs. But that was only part of the gruelling schedule. On top of the concerts there would be signings, Press interviews, photo shoots and promotions for every type of merchandise from Robbie pillowcases to Take That dolls. The fan club alone had 150,000 members. The band's second album, *Everything Changes*, had gone to number one and every one wanted a piece of them. For Rob, the dream of stardom had come true, but he didn't feel like a star. Surely, a star didn't get told off by his manager and treated like a naughty schoolboy for doing even the most innocuous rock'n'roll stuff, or get 150 quid-a-week and live with his mum. That wasn't Rob's idea of stardom. For him, stars were like Keith Moon, David Bowie or Bono. If being a star meant being like his nemesis Gary Barlow, you could keep it. Rob had been disgusted when Gary, who started to get royalty cheques for penning the band's early hits, chose to invest his money in a three-bedroom bungalow near his parent's home in Frodsham, Cheshire, and buy a sensible Ford Escort. If this was showbusiness Rob thought, he might as well have stuck to selling double glazing in Stoke. For Rob, Gary Barlow was the living embodiment of plastic pop, a man, he believed, more suited to flow charts and spread-sheets than raving. Barlow was never going to be found dead in a hotel room in a pool of his own vomit with a hooker and a bag of coke. 'I'm good with paying bills and saving' was the insight Gary gave his fans into his wild and crazy life in the band's official biography.

The cracks were beginning to show. Rob, a drinker since the days when barmen would slip him booze while his dad performed in the summer holiday camps, was becoming increasingly reliant on the bottle. Lager was his drink of choice, but he wasn't really fussy. There was also a new lure, drugs. As a kid in Stoke the boredom was relieved with cannabis and occasionally speed. Rob was even high when he took his GCSEs. He took his first line of coke before going on stage on Take That's first arena tour. By the end of 1994 the band was bigger than ever and on their way to selling £80-million worth of records around the world, but Martin-Smith was having problems with Rob. Always a smoker during the band's rise to the top, he had been repeatedly warned not to be photographed cigarette in hand, but he had begun taking less care. He had also taken to ignoring the ban on nights out in trendy clubs. While the four others were tucked up in bed or at least partying in private, Rob was getting slaughtered in upscale night spots. Nigel Martin-Smith lived in constant fear of him being photographed drunk or worse. Rob would stay out until 5 a.m. and his management took to sending a minder with him because he got into the habit of forgetting where he was. 'He wanted to lead his life the way he believed a star should enjoy himself. For Robbie it became all about the party,' remembers Martin-Smith. Fearful of the effects his newly rebellious star could have on the multi-million pound sponsorship deals, Martin-Smith began to get very worried. He had been responsible for creating the most controlled, most oiled and orchestrated pop group in British musical history and now it was all in danger of crashing down around his ears as Rob did his best to wreck everything. The manager was left incandescent when Rob pitched up to a band meeting with his hair dyed blue. This, after publicity shots for their new single had been done with Rob sporting blond locks. He had also begun his obsession with tattoos with a Maltese cross drawn on his hip.

On stage everything looked as normal. The band had started 1994 with promotional trips of Belgium, Germany and France and come back in time to rehearse their Beatles medley for the Brits where they picked up the Best Video award for "Pray". The European tour, which kicked off on March 24 in Hamburg and finished in Finland, had been a huge success. They returned to London to record *Top of the Pops* and caused mayhem when 3,000 'Thatters' turned up at their appearance on the Saturday morning show *Live And Kicking*. Rob had tried to look happy for Gary when he won two Ivor Novello awards in May for Songwriter of the Year and Best Contemporary Song for "Pray", but the tension between the two was apparent to all those around them. The *Pops Tour*, which kicked off in Glasgow in August, pushed Take That on to new heights, but Rob's behaviour on stage was beginning to bother his band mates and his manager. Martin-Smith was concerned that the once cheeky, cheery chap he had brought in to give the group a playful appeal, was turning into an aggressive scene-hogger. He was convinced it was either drink or drugs that was the cause of the change in the 20-year-old, but he was unsure what to do about it. The most important thing was to keep his troublesome heart-throb's problems out of the papers.

By the beginning of 1995, the situation was heading inexorably out of the hands of manager and band mates. To start with, Rob's voice was shot to pieces. The drinking, all night benders, coke and Ecstasy had wreaked havoc on it. By the time the band's third album, *Nobody Else*, was released in May, Rob's voice had been all but wiped from it. Unlike on the previous two, he was given no lead vocals and had sat bored and fidgeting throughout most of the recording sessions. His vocal omission didn't seem unduly to harm the finished product and it went double platinum in the first week of release.

But Nigel Martin-Smith could see his golden egg was in grave danger of cracking up. He had pulled Rob up about his behaviour on stage, not doing the moves the band had laboriously rehearsed, treating the whole evening like a sub-Robbie Williams concert. Martin-Smith accused Williams of upstaging his fellow Take That band mates and trying to steal the show. By now almost every showbusiness journalist in the land knew that Robbie Williams was spending more time with a bottle than his co-stars. He had even begun bragging of his drug-taking to a few of the writers from the daily tabloids who spent a lot of time around the band. As usual with Rob, though, his boasts were accompanied by a wicked glint of the eye, the 'is this a wind-up, or am I serious' look that has become his trademark, which is his way of beating everyone to the difficult question, defusing a situation with a knowing wink and the excuse that he was just having a laugh.

If Martin-Smith knew that this young guy, barely out of his teens, was in trouble why didn't he do something to help him? After all, had Take That not been in his own words 'a family'? The philosophy from the very outset had been 'us against the world', stick together and we can beat anyone.

Martin-Smith was, by early 1995, aware that Rob was drinking heavily. The dreaded first pictures had begun to appear in the pages of the tabloids of squeaky-clean boy band hunk Robbie Williams emerging bleary-eyed from nightclubs. He also started cropping up on television shows without the knowledge of his all-seeing, all-knowing manager. Martin-Smith told Take That's record company RCA that the boys would not be doing any more daytime TV shows as it was no longer, he felt, right for the band's image. He was furious when, the following day, the label's publicist, who had been keen to get the band on *This Morning*, rang to ask why, if they were not doing daytime television, was Rob to be seen on Channel Four with his mum in the VIP enclosure of Chester Races? In June, at the Nordoff Robbins Silver Clef awards in London's Intercontinental Hotel, Rob was at it again. Knocking back the complimentary white wine, he completely ignored Martin-Smith's instructions not to take part in the celebrity auction. While his Take That band mates watched silently, Rob bid £16,000 for a Wembley stadium ticket. This, as far as Rob was concerned, was rock'n'roll. The others could play by the rules if they wanted, but he was going to have some fun. On MTV he appeared wearing a T-shirt emblazoned with the words 'My Booze Hell'. Then, in front of 60 million European viewers, he accepted a £10 bet to moon live on air. The problem for Martin-Smith, as he desperately tried to paper over the cracks, was that if Robbie Williams was to be checked into rehab or a clinic you could guarantee the news would remain secret just long enough for a porter or fellow patient to pick up the phone to *The Sun*. The effect would be the same. Headlines screaming that teenybopper Take That singer Robbie Williams was being treated for drink and drug addiction would hardly fit with the image or please the companies who had hitched their wagons, at the cost of millions of pounds, to the clean-living lads from Manchester who were every granny's favourite.

Rob was a problem and so, as far as Martin-Smith was concerned, was Jan. Rob had always studiously ignored anything concerned with the business side of Take That and never bothered to keep an eye on their finances. During the band's twice-weekly business meetings to discuss strategy, Rob could barely contain his boredom. In 1994 the band, Martin-Smith and their advisors met executives from their record company RCA to renegotiate their contract with the label. The session went on for three hours and each person around the table was given a huge bundle of papers. At the end of the meeting Martin-Smith looked over at Rob's untouched pile of papers. On the top sheet was drawn a picture of a huge pair of breasts and signed 'Rob'. But Jan was very interested in her son's finances. She had run her own business and was only too aware of the rip-offs that had been perpetrated on previous bands down the years by their managers. She was horrified when Rob told her he under-stood little of the information he was given by his management team. Jan had been a co-signatory to all Rob's contracts because, when he had joined the band, he was still a minor. So, with Rob's backing, Jan set about the task of discovering just how much Rob had earned and how much he was seeing of his money. She went to see the band's accountants to question them about her son's finances. When word of her investigations got back to Martin-Smith all hell broke loose. Rob, in Australia with the band at the time in the summer of 1994, only found out about the furore back home when he got into the hotel lift with the other boys one morning. The relationship between star and manager was now irretrievable.

CHAPTER FOUR
mad for it

T'ake That tour manager Chris Healey leafed through a handful of scrawled A4 pages then picked up the phone in his office and dialled Nigel Martin-Smith's number. 'I've got something here I think you should see,' he said. Two hours earlier in the unlikely setting of a Territorial Army barracks in Stockport, Cheshire, amid scenes of bitterness and recrimination, Robbie Williams's career as boy band member had come to an end.

The group were meant to be rehearsing for a tour that would cost £2 million to stage. But Rob didn't want to do it. He told Martin-Smith and his fellow members of the band that he would give them the agreed six months' notice and then he would be gone. But now, in these distinctly unglamorous surroundings, critical mass had been reached. There was dispute to follow about whether Rob jumped or was pushed. What did it matter? He was out. There was no going back and it would be only a matter of time before the band, holed below the waterline, would be gone as well.

It's the sort of hypothetical poser they put to Prada-suited

PRs over muffins and skinny lattes at £5,000-a-head confer-
ences for the country's top image-makers: You've got a
21-year-old member of a boy band who wants to go solo. The
band is squeaky clean to appeal to its teenage girl fans. But the
fans are getting older and your client needs a new, hipper,
more rebellious image to win a more mature market. Discuss.

Post Robbie Williams's split from Take That, the stock
answer is probably: get your man an expensive drink and
drugs addiction, send him to Glastonbury, make sure he is
photographed completely out of his tree and put him on
stage with the meanest, nastiest, most foul-mouthed rockers
in the land. The downside, of course, is that your pop star
will have virtually to drown in a mire of self-pity and the
bottle for 12 months, come within a whisker of flushing
what is left of his career down the toilet and self-destruct on
the pages of every newspaper. But hey, that's showbiz. Oh,
and by the way, it would be even better if, during this year-
long public battle with his demons, your boy could see his
way clear to writing a modern classic about redemption and
forgiveness for the re-launch.

If Rob had sat down and planned his transformation from
fresh-faced, but uncool teen idol, to narcotics-fuelled bad
boy with attitude, he couldn't have done it better. The
moment he staggered on stage with Oasis on June 23, 1995,
was his own Road to Damascus conversion. Drunk on a
heady mix of nicked champagne and freedom, he'd gone out
there in front of 110,000 cynical rock fans as another prat
from a boy band and left the stage the latest New Lad
Britpopper. Earlier that day, at a charity event with Take
That, Rob had told Nigel Martin-Smith he wanted to go to

the annual rock festival. At this point Rob was still playing the game – just about. He knew 'Take That Towers' rules specified that he needed permission from his manager if he wanted to appear in public without the rest of the band. Had Rob made the same request, even a short while earlier, he could be pretty sure the answer from his Svengali boss would have been short and to the point. But now the situation was different, Rob was different. There was a new steeliness about him. Martin-Smith put it down to the drugs he knew his young star was taking, but he also knew that Rob probably only needed a push in the right direction to tell the man who'd turned him into one of the most famous faces in the land to stick it. In hindsight, Martin-Smith is aware that that moment was pivotal. He has subsequently rebuked himself for going along with the whole thing too long, for papering over the cracks, but in the early summer of 1995 he still thought he could hold the whole thing together. He had controlled these boys for so long, telling them what to eat, where to go and what to say. His mistake was thinking he could continue to pull it off with Rob.

The signs of Rob's disillusionment had been on display for some time. He really didn't want to know any more. He had been a disruptive element while recording and wasn't bothering to learn the dance moves, criticizing them, saying they were embarrassing. 'They're your moves not mine,' he had told the other four. A month earlier, in a blatant act of defiance, he had broken the band's 'no girlfriends' rule by arriving at Take That's end-of-tour bash with ex-*London's Burning* star Samantha Beckinsale. So on June 23, as he went through the motions of being a Take That member, he was ready for a fight. Martin-Smith, sensing problems, was prepared to compromise. Rob could go to Glastonbury, but he would have to take one of the band's minders to make sure no photographs of him enjoying the gig could end up in the papers. The edict did nothing to improve Rob's humour. He wasn't going to turn up among the rockers and hippies holding hands with some bodyguard. He could already hear the taunts from the bands he admired and wanted to befriend, the jibes about not being allowed out by himself in case he got lost and couldn't find his way home to his clean-living chums.

As far as Rob was concerned Nigel could like it or lump it. He wasn't going to take a minder. He remembers little else about that sunny Friday. He can still recall filling a borrowed blacked-out Jag with 16 bottles of champagne from the do and being driven down the A39 to Somerset. By the time he arrived he was down to 15 bottles and ready to rave. As he pulled up backstage and opened up the boot to unload his bubbly, Rob was met by Liam Gallagher. 'Take fucking what?' was the Mancunian's considered greeting. As far as Rob was concerned, what Liam lacked in erudition he made up for in attitude. One of the primary reasons for making the trip and disobeying his manager was so that he could meet Liam and his brother Noel. They were the back-bone of Britain's coolest band, the leaders of Britpop and makers of great records. They had everything Rob wanted for himself: the in-your-face swagger, the street savvy, the rock'n'roll sleaze. Rob was where he wanted to be, having his picture taken with the other Britpop titans Blur, playing football with The Boo Radleys, signing autographs 'Robbie

Williams, nutter', giving drunken interviews to anyone who asked, letting the paparazzi do their worst. He was painfully aware of how his fellow revellers viewed him. 'People looked at me like I was a zit on the end of their nose because I'm a member of Take That. They think I'm a total prat,' he said at the time. Three songs into Oasis's headlining set, Liam shouted 'Come on' to Rob who was standing at the side of the Pyramid stage. A moment later, looking like a naughty nephew who's gone round a family party finishing everyone's leftovers, Rob was lurching into the lights and out of a job. Front-tooth blacked out, he became Oasis's most famous groupie, simultaneously giving a massive bicep-clutching salute to his four co-workers and their manager. Rob might have been completely loaded, off his head on booze and adrenalin, but even in that haze of chemicals he knew this was something momentous, a new direction, a new chapter. 'That was the moment it actually crystallized' would be his abiding memory.

For those around the Take That star, who weren't as completely obliterated as he was, the sight of this public metamorphosis was not easy to watch. A library of Press images charts the course of that day, his initiation as a fully-fledged, fully-loaded rock star. Rob would later claim the trip had been an exercise in PR, a statement of intent, but one picture in particular makes very difficult viewing. Rob, swollen-faced, on his back, peroxide hair in the grass, the soles of his white Adidas trainers showing, his legs in dark jeans bent at the knee. His glassy eyes are caught by the flash, his left arm is raised off the ground, trying to point at the cameraman, acknowledging he knows his picture is being taken and somehow, even in his out-of-it state, he is aware that this there is something wrong with this situation, that certain liberties are being taken, but there's not a damn thing he can do about it. When it came to drink and drugs, the ship had sailed on Rob's innocence some long time since, but being faced with the undeniable evidence over breakfast the following morning would come as something of a shock to his millions of schoolgirl fans. They, of course, were no longer top of Rob's agenda.

Rob loves to recall how he arrived at Glastonbury in a limo and left in the back of a van. He had made friends with Oasis sidekick and good-time boy Tim Abbott and got himself a lift back to Jan's house in Stoke in the back of their roadies' Transit van. The choice of transport is, Williams believes, symbolic; the pampered, prissy, cloistered, up-town world of Take That giving way to good, old-fashioned, scuzzy, sweaty, rock'n'roll. It would sum up the next two years of his life, Rob later claimed.

Had the pop world just fallen victim to the most astutely pulled-off stunt in a business known for them? Is it possible that the whole episode had been a charade, orchestrated by a man schooled in the black arts of spin and publicity since he was 16? A year later Rob would claim: 'I was at Glastonbury for a reason. Primarily, I was there for effect, and also to meet the Oasis lads. I hadn't been allowed to do interviews or photos without someone from the record company around me, so I thought, "Right, you'd better look at me now because I've turned a different corner." I made sure I did every interview and I made sure I did every photo shoot, every cameraman got a picture of me. And I made

Second Mum: Baby Robbie
with his elder sister
Sally who helped take
care of her little brother.

"Fatsykins": Chubby
Robbie was teased
about his weight
by other kids, but
it won him acting roles.

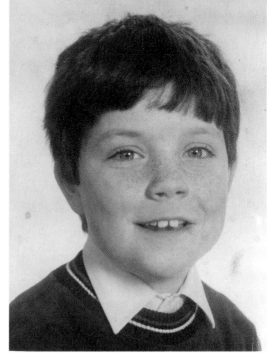

Hairly Days: A permed 15-year-old Robbie checks out some tunes.

No.1 Fan: Robbie with his adored grandmother Betty Williams. After her death he wrote 'Nan's Song' for her.

Class Clown: Grinning Rob loved acting the fool, but hated lessons.

Class Act: Rob's school year picture at St Margaret Ward School in Tunstall.

Mr Popular: Robbie found that making girls laugh got him dates.

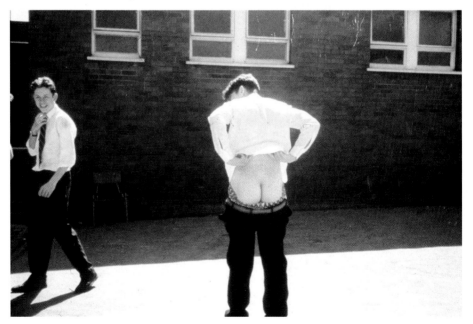

Come Undone: Rob's trousers head south in a playground prank that became his trademark.

Chip Off The Old Block: Robbie inherited
his showman genes from his comic dad Pete.

Hat's My Boy: Rob and his beloved mum Jan.

Cool Dude: Rob at Camarthen Bay in 1990, the day he heard he had won an audition for Take That.

Brothers In Arms: Despite the hugs, Take That were never close friends.

Just Take That: Robbie does his famous impression of Tommy Cooper while Jason, Mark, Gary and Howard do their best to put him off.

Pretty Boys: Take That had to dump their gay image when girls discovered them.

Starmaker: Nigel Martin-Smith was the man behind Take That, but Robbie grew to hate him.

Suits You: Take That wow the fans in a Royal Variety performance, November 1994.

Mad For It: Robbie made a new pal in Liam Gallagher at Glastonbury 1995, but the pair fell out in spectacular style.

Blacked-out: Rob covered up a tooth for a laugh at Glastonbury, but passed out later after a champagne binge.

sure I did every interview pissed as well.' The strategy was high-risk. There's a fine line between fun-loving wild man and sad, drunken loser, chucking his career down the toilet. If this was the first salvo in a PR war from which Rob would emerge the undisputed winner a little over two years later, it was, without doubt, one of the shrewdest pieces of marketing in the history of pop, especially when the conductor of the campaign was regularly sinking two bottles of vodka a day.

At home in Hale, Cheshire, Nigel Martin-Smith was settling down to a night in front of the television. He was greeted by the sight of one-fifth of his £80 million investment acting like a nutcase in front of the world's media.

The following Monday, back in rehearsals for the upcoming UK tour, Rob, with schoolkid eagerness, couldn't wait to give chapter and verse of his exploits to his Take That colleagues. His four fellow stars, with the undisguised disdain of those left off the party list, were not a willing audience. Anyway, they knew all about it already. The situation deteriorated a few days later over a curry with the band and Martin-Smith. While the prospect of legal action was on the cards, Rob was admitting nothing, but the truth is he had already decided to leave and told his band mates so. But his plan was to give them their six months' notice while he decided how to get his solo career going. He had told Jan of his plans and she had already got to work as Rob's new unofficial manager, sounding out contacts and giving them the nod that her son was about to jump ship and would be available for work. Although the signs had been there for some time, the moment, when it came, was a shock to Take

That and Martin-Smith. There had been an expectation that Rob would get over his restlessness. Who in their right mind would leave a band that was on its way to selling 20 million records and was the biggest pop group of its time?

On Thursday July 13, 1995, matters came to a head. Rob was showing little inclination to get to grips with the choreography for the 20-date UK tour that would kick off in Manchester in a little over two weeks' time. He would admit later that he needed a bottle of vodka before he could go into rehearsals with the band and could only cope with his feelings of dejection afterwards by getting completely slaughtered. He was already a fully blown alcoholic and drug addict. Rob was, at best, going through the motions. At worst, he was becoming a poltergeist, upsetting the atmosphere, demob-happy, waiting for the £1 million cheque at the end of the tour. Typically, he couldn't resist winding up his band mates about the cheesy dance moves and the crappy outfits. The other four were fed up with him and, more importantly, so was Martin-Smith. The tour could not be jeopardized by Rob walking out in the middle of it. Even if he left now the marketing campaign would be damaged, and merchandising would be hit – Robbie was on all the posters. To complicate things even more, Take That had just signed a £1-million deal with Arista Records in the US. Martin-Smith confronted Rob and asked him to commit to the band. The conversation did not go well. 'I don't want to be one of Gary Barlow's backing dancers,' was his reply. 'I'll come to rehearsals and I'll be there, but I'll do it my way.'

Perhaps it is apt that the bleak, institutional surroundings of a Territorial Army camp should be the location of Rob's final scenes with Take That. Later, he would compare his five years with the band to being in the Forces: controlled, told what to eat, what to drink, what to think, who to be seen with, where to go, every moment of every day planned for him with military precision. Over lunch, the bitterness and resentment erupted. Rob maintained he was fired. Certainly he had not gone into that room that day with the intention of emerging Robbie Williams, ex-Take That member.

The unlikely brinksman, Williams claimed, was Jason Orange who told Rob the band planned to prove they could hack it as a four-piece 'now and not later'. Rob claimed he was stunned by the statement. Wrong-footed and shocked, the cockiness took over. 'Fine, if that's the way you want it,' hit back Rob. He picked up the piece of melon he was eating and sarcastically asked if he could keep it. Silently, he collected his stuff together as his band mates watched. Then the couldn't-care-less mask slipped. The realization of what was happening hit home and, like a dead man walking, Rob suddenly wanted the Governor's reprieve. In the stare-out contest Rob was the one to blink. At the door, he turned and addressed his band partners. 'Look, I'm going. No coming back. This is it,' he said. Take That was a foursome. The others looked at him blankly and Rob was gone.

In the car with his driver Paul and minder Chris, Rob sat silently. When they dropped him off, Paul told Rob he would pick him up same time tomorrow. Rob told his driver he wasn't coming back. Confused, the driver said he would collect him on Thursday instead. 'No, Paul, you don't understand,' said a weeping Rob. 'I'm not coming back, ever.'

The remaining members of Take That insisted the decision

to leave the band had been Rob's and that they had told him to go away and think about it. In an immediate showbusiness declaration of freedom, Rob did his thinking in the company of George Michael, Paula Yates and Michael Hutchence in St Tropez. George was throwing a lavish party at his south of France home to celebrate his new £60-million record deal with Virgin. Rob, newly anointed member of the hip set, was on the guest list. There, he told his new chums about his, yet to be publicly announced, departure from the band and asked George for his advice. The star, who had gone through his own boy band extrication in 1986, gave the move his blessing. One person Rob didn't inform of his exit from the band was his dad. The first thing Pete knew about it was when a fan rang in tears to plead with him: 'Tell me it's not true.' Pete tried to get hold of his son, but Rob's phone was off the hook. Partying with the glitterati on the Med succeeded in distracting Rob from the reality of what had happened, but not for long. He returned to the UK and into the lion's den. Word of his split from Take That was out.

Even by Take That standards, the level of hysteria that greeted the news – it was revealed in *The Sun* on July 18 that Robbie was no longer in the band – was an eye-opener. Slack-jawed 'Thatters' roamed the streets in varying states of distress. In Hamburg, Frau Sylvia Tegtmeier's 14-year-old daughter Sabrina and her friend told her they were going to throw themselves in front of a moving lorry. When the local radio station N-Joy announced the news, they received more than a thousand calls, many from teenagers threatening suicide. In Britain, the airwaves were full of weeping fans and at the London offices of gay magazine *Boyz*, staff wore black for a week. 'Robbie was everyone's favourite,' said editor Simon Gage. 'At least him and Jason. And Mark ... well, all of them except Howard.' Special phone hotlines were set up to minister to the grieving.

Rob was first out of the blocks in the post-split publicity battle. He was already planning to sue his bosses RCA and Martin-Smith and he was on the attack. He claimed he had been thinking of leaving the group for a year because he was sick of toeing the party line, tired of living in a 'cocoon' 24-hours-a-day, seven-days-a-week. 'I was kept away from reality,' he complained. At 16 he was prepared to accept the conditioning to become a pop star, 'I wanted it and accepted it,' he said. But Rob maintained that Martin-Smith was wrong to continue the same treatment of a 21-year-old. He had realized on Take That's last European tour that, despite the tour's success and the money that was rolling in, he was unhappy. 'I'd actually been kidding myself I was happy for months, but deep down I'd had enough. I had grown out of it and needed and wanted something else,' he said. Being on stage with Take That had not been like being in a band. In fact, out there in front of the fans, his over-riding emotion was loneliness. And, while the four others were seeking to put a positive spin on the split, desperate not to dent the nicey-nicey Take That image and still peddling the line that they had parted the best of friends, Rob was delivering a few home truths. 'The fans think they know the guys, but they don't,' he said. 'No one does. We used to tell people in inter-views that if we weren't in Take That we would still have been mates. Well, I'm sorry to say that just isn't true. What we had was strictly business.' In a prelude to the hostilities to come, Rob said that, despite living and working with Gary Barlow almost every day for five years, he still felt he didn't know him. He would feel immediately uncomfortable if he had to sit next to Gary on a flight. He had desperately wanted them all to be close, but the relationship between all five had been strange from the beginning. They had never, he revealed, had a fight. 'The five of us never argued and I can see now that's unhealthy,' he said. 'It was against the rules and we just bottled it up.' Rob, who had recently been spending his time writing poetry, had never written a Take That song. The management were not interested. Gary was the songwriter, Robbie the cheeky one, that's the way it would always be. Now Rob wanted to record his own songs, not sing Barlow's lines anymore.

Chris Healey was still taking in the news that Rob had walked out of the rehearsal rooms and out of the band that afternoon. As the Take That tour manager absent-mindedly sifted through some papers in his office, he came across the abandoned sheets. He recognized the handwriting as Rob's and read through the lyrics to two songs. He was reading them for a second time when he got Nigel Martin-Smith on the line. 'They're bloody good,' he told his boss. 'The songs were about me and the other boys and how unhappy he was,' said Martin-Smith. 'When I saw them I was gob-smacked. They were clever lyrics.'

CHAPTER FIVE
fall-out

Kevin Kinsella is described by those who know him as 'a character'. He is probably described by those who don't know him as 'a right nutter'. Born in Ireland and brought up in west London, he is a former boxer who became involved in the music business in the 1960s. Like the comedian Ken Dodd, his hair stands on end, though not, you suspect, with any comedic intention. He is likely to sport half-mast trousers, paired with multi-coloured stripy socks.

Early in 1995 Granada Television contacted Kinsella, a Manchester-based celebrity fixer and independent record label boss, to see if he could secure getting Robbie Williams to front his own chat show in Malibu which would be called *Robbie on the Beach*. Granada was all too aware that the most charismatic and talkative member of Take That would make for great television. The problem, Kinsella pointed out to the television executives, was that Robbie Williams was still in Take That. But Kinsella had a contact who knew Rob's mum, Jan, and a meeting was arranged between the two.

When he approached Jan, Rob's mother was playing a

bigger and bigger part in her son's career. Her involvement had already caused her to fall out with Nigel Martin-Smith. Within the Take That hierarchy her name was mud. She was, as far as they were concerned, the archetypal pushy mother, a parent who put her son into the spotlight, wrote out his CV herself, told him how to enter and leave a room, controlled and moulded him and then bit the hand that fed her ungrateful offspring. Jan Williams told Kinsella that Rob would be interested in the TV idea, but he was a Take That member and bound to Nigel Martin-Smith. It was then, says Kinsella, that Jan confided to him that, although for the moment, Rob was still in the band, he wouldn't be for more than a few months more. The deal with Granada could be a possibility when Rob was out of Take That. Kinsella next heard from Mrs Williams sooner than he had expected. In mid-July, Jan rang to say that Robert, as she always calls him, was no longer a member of Take That. He was in a bad way and had gone to spend time at George Michael's house. He would be flying back into Manchester and would Kinsella be prepared to take him on and act as his new manager?

Kevin Kinsella's first meeting with Robert Williams was to sum up the star's state of mind for the length of their involvement. Kevin had driven to Ringway Airport with Jan to collect Rob from his flight from France. Within seconds of getting into Kinsella's car, rock's new wildman, christened on the fields of Glastonbury, was in floods of tears. 'He broke down in the car,' says Kinsella today. 'He was in a bloody terrible state.' Kinsella drove Rob to his home in Knutsford, Cheshire, where he would remain off and on for the next four months. Looking back, it is clear to Kevin that Rob's world was in free fall. 'He was weeping for his career, for the life he had in that band,' he says. 'All he had ever wanted was fame, to be well known and spotted in the street. Now he was in danger of losing it all and he was terrified.'

Jan's choice of Kinsella as the man to rebuild Robbie Williams's career was greeted with some scepticism in the music business. Yes, Kinsella, had dealt with stars like Lisa Stansfield, but he was not considered a big shot. Surely, they thought, a member of the biggest pop band in Europe could find someone who was a recognized player. But, says Kinsella now, his new manager had only ever planned to take on the ex-boy-band star in the short term. His plan was to keep Rob out of the way until his confused client had a chance to get his head together and decide what he wanted to do next. Reporters and TV crews arrived outside Kinsella's house hoping to get a sighting of the runaway teen idol. Kinsella sent them away saying he didn't know where he was. Rob, meanwhile, was playing football in the back garden with Kinsella's son, Kevin Jnr. Elsewhere, the hunt for the missing Take That refugee was in full swing. There had been sightings, it was claimed, at Carmarthen Bay Holiday Camp, where his dad Pete worked. Take That fans were so sure their hero was hiding out there that, under cover of darkness, they plundered site manager Andrew Brown's Y-fronts from his washing line, convinced they belonged to Rob. At the same time newspaper executives in Wapping were preparing to make a £250,000 bid to the star for the full story of his departure from the band.

Rob was not in good shape. During those first, dark few weeks after the split, he spent much of his time in tears or slumped on Kinsella's sofa, drunk and drugged up. His new landlords were regularly greeted by the sight of Rob sprawled there all day in just his Calvin Klein underpants. Rob would lie in bed until lunchtime and then begin the business of getting quickly and completely pissed. 'He would drink two bottles of vodka a day. Rob would send out my daughter to buy it,' says Kinsella. 'He had a phenomenal capacity to put it away.' Days were spent drinking and running up a huge bill on Kinsella's phone. 'He was going through a breakdown,' says Kinsella. 'He had been kicked out of Take That and he had no idea what to do with himself. Being famous had been his life since he was teenager. It is what he did. I really don't believe he knew how to be a real person. He was terrified by the idea of it.'

Kinsella, as his new manager, had a problem. His star was in meltdown, but he was there to manage his career and, despite having £1.5 million in the bank from his time with Take That, Rob wanted to get out there in the spotlight again, prove he was still a star and show that he didn't need the band any more. But one look at him could have told those around him that he was far from ready for the fray. Rob was also not having the PR campaign all his own way. Less than a month after he walked out of the band, the *Daily Star* splashed claims that Robbie Williams had taken drugs. The banner headline read: 'Take That Sensation: We Had To Sack Drugs Daft Robbie.' Immediately on the defensive, Rob's lawyer quickly announced he was threatening to sue the paper, which reported that the star's performances had suffered because he was taking cocaine and Ecstasy. The paper had also claimed his management had tried to get the singer to seek professional help. Robbie was said by his legal team to be 'horrified and angry'. 'I have read the article, which is untrue,' said his solicitor Graham Shear. Kevin Kinsella was also pouring scorn on the claims. 'To my knowledge he has never touched anything, not even aspirin,' he was quoted as saying at the time. Bizarrely, the press office at RCA was now handling Take That's PR as well as Robbie Williams, solo artist.

At the same time, Kinsella signed Rob up for a guest presenter's spot, sitting in for Lily Savage, on Channel Four's *The Big Breakfast*. The track of television presenting had long been predicted for Williams, and Kinsella felt the £100,000 slot would give his new client the exposure he needed and wanted. But during a Press call to announce his new post, things looked far from well. A month out of the shackles of Take That and the strain was beginning to show. Rob was already noticeably podgier and paler. The Press would describe his performance for them as 'excitable', perhaps due to the fact that Rob had needed a hit of cocaine before arriving at the show's East London studios. As Kinsella drove Rob there, he suddenly panicked. 'I can't do it. I just can't go through with it,' he told his manager. Kinsella spent the next 20 minutes desperately trying to persuade his reluctant star he had to honour his commitment to appear on the show. 'We had been paid up front,' says Kinsella.

Eventually, a tearful Rob agreed and once in front of the cameras, Robbie, the Williams alter ego, was switched on. Twice taking off his trousers and turning the air blue with a string of near-the-knuckle gags, it was obvious the Take That rulebook had been torn up once and for all. Pouring tea into a huge cup for the cameras and wearing a *Big Breakfast* football-style shirt, Robbie was on form. But the look didn't scream 'pop star'. With his close-cropped hair and long side-burns over jowly cheeks, the effect was more Amish *Fat Club*. Openly smoking in front of his female fans, he said he was planning to 're-invent' himself. But, below the surface, the insecurities were there too. Perhaps trying to convince himself more than the viewing public, he added: 'I don't need to work. I am Robbie Williams all the time for a living.'

But, being Robbie Williams was taking its toll on Rob. He had started spending time in the company of the then Liverpool goalkeeper, David James. James, himself not adverse to clubbing and drinking, had earned the unenvi-able tag at Anfield as a member of "The Spice Boys", the high-living and glamorous set of Liverpool stars who could party as well as they played. James was a regular visitor to Kinsella's home to pick up his famous pal for nights out in Liverpool and Manchester. Kinsella had tagged along once, but subsequently refused to get in a car with James behind the wheel after the goalie terrified him with his foot-to-the-floor driving style. To outsiders, the star might have appeared to be living the high-life now he had got rid of his Take That chaperones, but the reality was far from the case. Kinsella was becoming increasingly worried by Rob's state of mind, plus his addiction to cocaine and particularly alcohol. 'Rob had absolutely nothing to say if he wasn't pissed,' says Kinsella. 'He was known as the cheeky, fun one in Take That, always joking, but to be honest he was incred-ibly dull to be around. He was a very boring man. He had very few interests. His whole life was showbiz or the things that go with it. He would constantly drone on about how much Versace was charging him for a suit or something, but he had nothing to say about anything important. His life was just totally shallow.'

Kinsella was convinced Williams was using the bottle and drugs in order to be able to face the world, as though he had to be off his face in order to deal with people, to be able to put on the Robbie mask. 'He loved to have people around him,' says Kinsella. 'He wanted a group of hangers-on with him as if he felt that it would prove to himself that he was popular. If he was sober he would have been too intimidated to be around them. I think he felt he was pretty worthless and uninteresting and needed to be out of it to think he was having a good time.' His manager believed that the 21-year-old was facing the biggest identity crisis of his life. 'He was completely confused about who he was and how he was going to live his life,' says Kinsella. 'I believe some very unpleasant things happened to him when he was in that band. He was very young, just a kid, when he joined and he was deeply scarred by what had happened to him. He broke down and told me about how confused he was. He was very open, he told me everything. The kid was a mess. It was not just his career, it was his personal life too. He was trying to come to terms with everything that had happened to him. It was impossible not to feel very sorry for him.'

Kinsella says he also became aware of a tension in Rob's relationship with his family. 'At that time I had not met his father, but I had many dealings with Jan and his sister Sally,' he says. 'Because of the situation he was in, I think he needed to be away from Jan for a time.' Their relationship, says Kinsella, was incredibly close. But his manager felt it was too intense for the good of his client's health. 'At that time, I believe Rob wanted to get away from his mum and that's why he moved in with me and my family. I think he wanted some stability, but needed space from her.' As a result there was almost immediate tension between manager and mother. 'Jan is very controlling of Rob,' says Kinsella. 'She is the boss in that relationship. She had run her own business, had learnt a lot about the pop business and she was taking a much bigger part in his work. She is a tough cookie. She liked the glamour and money of her son's fame, but she always wanted to be in control.'

The balance of power in the mother–son relationship was never more glaringly obvious than when Kinsella accompanied Rob and Jan to a meeting with lawyers in London. In true rock-star fashion the singer was in demanding mode. 'Rob suddenly announced in the middle of the meeting that he wanted some sushi,' recalls Kinsella. 'He was always doing stuff like this. It didn't seem to enter his head this was a legal firm, not a bloody Japanese restaurant. As far as he was concerned he was a pop star so whatever he wanted he got. But Jan was having none of it. She just turned to him and said, "No, you can have some later." It was like watching a mum telling a schoolboy he couldn't have any sweets.' Rob, the strutting millionaire, kept quiet. 'He didn't dare say anything else,' says Kinsella. 'Whenever they were talking about business Jan would speak to Rob very, very slowly like she was talking to a complete fool.' The tension between Jan and Kinsella would come to a head when Rob, who had become very close to his adopted family, told Jan he considered Kinsella to be 'like a father to me'. 'At that very moment,' say Kevin.

'I knew that was the end of my relationship with Rob. I thought there was no way Jan was going to stand for having anyone that close to her son. That was her territory. She couldn't even pretend. She actually said she was devastated that Rob had said that. She couldn't tolerate not being in complete control of him.' Kinsella also had little time for Rob's elder sister, Sally, who, the star says, was his surrogate mum when he was growing up. 'They are always painted as having such a great relationship,' he says. 'But they fought like cat and dog. They were up and down all the time. Often he wouldn't speak to her for weeks. But, like Jan, she was part of the set-up. She made her living out of Rob. She got paid very well by him to run his fan club,' he adds.

At the end of August Rob came face to face with his ex-Take That colleagues for the first time since he walked out of the Stockport barracks. The 'reunion' took place at the *National Television Awards* in London. The boys did no more than wave at each other, but it was enough to leave Rob traumatized. He was found wandering backstage weeping. 'It feels so weird,' he was quoted as saying. 'But I know I've got to start a new life.' There seemed to be very little strategy though. Shouldn't the wannabe 'serious' musician have been locked away with notepad and guitar writing the songs that would show the world he was more than just a poster boy and grinning dancer? Instead, bizarrely, he signed up as the £100,000 'freaky face' of 7-up Light. Nothing particularly strange about pop stars getting paid loads of money to promote fizzy drinks. But how many others don a black wig, bikini bottoms and stilettos for a poster advert and pose for the Press in said outfit with six similarly dressed models?

What exactly, other than adding to his bank account, was this doing for Rob's much vaunted re-invention?

Rob had made an attempt to record some of his own material in his manager's Manchester studio. The verdict from Kinsella was not hopeful. 'It was shit,' Kevin says now. Meanwhile, Kinsella was hard at work trying to find a way to get Rob out of his contract with Take That's record company RCA. It was blatantly obvious to him and Rob that there was no way Rob, as a solo performer, could stay on the same label as his ex-colleagues. As far as he was concerned there was a massive conflict of interest. What Robbie Williams, solo performer, needed was a new company who didn't see him as ex-boy-band star, but would build him as a mature singer in his own right. Also, both Rob and Kinsella were under no illusion about where RCA's priorities would lie if Take That called it a day and Gary Barlow emerged to launch the solo career half the entertainment world had been predicting for 18 months. This label just wasn't big enough for the both of them.

Two months after the split, Rob was fighting a battle for his sanity. In public, he would admit: 'It's not been good. It's not good now. It has been bad. I've just got to find something for myself now that makes me feel good about myself again, because I don't feel great about myself right now.' In private, he was panicking. He would admit that he had played the part of Robbie Williams for so long, he didn't actually know who Rob was any more. Later he would say: 'I didn't know what to do with myself. I believed I had no other function than being in Take That.'

Yes, he had been very unhappy in Take That. He had

wanted out for some time. He didn't miss the rules, the other boys or the dreaded Martin-Smith. What he hadn't bargained for was the completely, overwhelmingly debilitating effect of having all that adulation taken away. He had moaned about landing at yet another airport to be greeted by yet another set of screaming fans. There had been times when he'd lost his patience with the girls doorstepping his mum's house. His dad had, more than once, to talk him out of telling the more determined 'Thatters' to 'eff off. But now he missed it. The fundamental fact was then, and remains today, that Williams without the crutch of the adoration of others is robbed of his spirit, his reason to be, the whole point of him. Denied his life-blood on Kevin Kinsella's living room sofa, only the anaesthetic of white powder and neat alcohol could keep at bay the physical pain of its loss. On a shopping trip to Milan he was greeted by 3,000 girl fans at the airport. 'I cried and cried because it felt so good,' said Rob. 'I really miss the adulation. In Take That I became so blasé about it, but you don't know what you're got until it's gone.' Later he would admit: 'My world came to an end for a while there and there were times I thought I'd never be happy again.'

At the same time, and possibly because of Rob's fragile state, the gloves were coming off in the cold war that followed Rob's exit from Take That. On August 8, Rob issued a statement through his solicitor Jack Rabinowicz reiterating the reasons why he had decided to leave the band. He accused Martin-Smith of not being 'even-handed' in his treatment of him and described himself as still being a member of the band even though he admitted it was unlikely he would perform with them again. The move was important in his legal strategy. The plan drawn up between Rob, Kinsella and his lawyers was that he would claim he had been sacked from the band and this would open up the way for a case of constructive dismissal. Once again, his ex-band mates tried to remain aloof from the mud-slinging. They were 'extremely upset' by Rob's claims, but would always 'love him as a friend' no matter what he said or did. In public, at least, Rob, too, was endeavouring to continue the pretence that he had not fallen out with the other four, but his lawyer admitted: 'Robbie's friendship with Nigel and the others has paled significantly in recent weeks.'

It was clear that he was desperately trying to find out who the hell he was. He told journalists he wanted to get a girl-friend, buy a tumble-dryer and spend more time at home. But his choice of words presented a *prima facie* case that he was no nearer to answering this fundamental question. 'I'm not going to find the real Robbie Williams jetting off to New York. I'm going to find him at home where he hasn't been for six years,' he said. Somewhere in the intervening years since he was plucked from obscurity by Nigel Martin-Smith, Rob from Stoke seemed to have been subjugated, trampled and crushed by the Robbie bandwagon, overtaken by the character he had willingly colluded in creating with his now ex-manager. What was left was a showman without a show.

Given his state, it was perhaps less than well advised to throw the delicate star into the lion's den. Kevin Kinsella thought he had come up with a good photo opportunity when he agreed to Rob appearing in a five-a-side football game during the half-time interval at Stoke City's local derby with Rob's beloved Port Vale. What Kinsella hadn't bargained for was the level of hostility from the City fans to their bitter rival's most celebrated supporter. Rob was against the idea but, persuaded by his manager, he was driven through the crowd for his appearance before the 13,000-strong crowd. As they crawled into the car park, Rob panicked. 'They'll kill me,' he told Kinsella. 'Don't be fucking stupid,' was Kinsella's less than sympathetic response. 'You don't know these people,' came the terrified Williams reply. As he was introduced to Stoke's Victoria Ground faithful, Rob was greeted with boos and hisses and chants of 'Take That reject'. Rob kept a fixed, smiling mask, but ducked out of the game. He was devastated by his treatment at the hands of the fans. Kinsella was unsympathetic. 'I couldn't believe he was being such a baby,' he says. 'He was wetting himself. He actually thought those people were going to kill him, he was so paranoid.' For Kinsella, the incident served to highlight the difference between the pop star swagger, the ball-breaking confidence of the Robbie Williams persona and the reality of Rob the person. 'In reality Rob was never able to deal with confrontation,' says Kinsella. 'If he was ever in a position where someone was in his face, Rob would back away. He never felt comfortable in those situations. His reaction would always be to shy away. The impression he gives is of this tough-talking guy with the fuck-you attitude, but it is an act, it's all part of the Robbie Williams façade.'

While the wrangling about Rob's deal with RCA and his 'sacking' was cranking up, both Rob and Kinsella agreed that it would suit a pop star, who was keen to get himself talked about, to be in London. Rob had never been that keen on Manchester and, anyway, his new Brit pop chums like Noel and Liam were having it large in the capital. London was definitely the place to be. Rob set off with Kinsella's son Kevin Jnr in tow, eager to sample the pop star life that had been denied him by Nigel Martin-Smith's code of conduct. Rob was determined to live it to the max; no invite would be declined, no premier unattended. With the zeal of a convert, Rob let out his new battle cry: 'Let's party'.

As lawyers began preparing his case and Kinsella began talks with Virgin to take the new solo Robbie Williams to the label, Rob was making up for lost time, drinking with Noel and Liam, propping up the bar at the ultra-hip Atlantic Bar and Grill. Less than a month into his relocation and his fervour for the nocturnal attractions of the city was starting to show. Back home in Cheshire, Kinsella got a phone call from his friend and top record producer Nellee Hooper. Hooper, the former Soul II Soul producer, who has worked with some of the biggest names in pop including Madonna, was acutely aware of the pitfalls facing the young, rich and famous and what he saw in Rob's behaviour sent a chill down his spine. His message to Kinsella was simple: 'Get Rob out of London or he'll be dead in three months.' Kinsella knew from his son that Rob's high living had gone up a gear since his arrival in London and he took seriously the warning from a man who had seen it all before. 'Rob had gone off the rails completely,' says Kinsella. 'He was drinking even more and putting thousands of pounds up his nose. Nellee knows the music business. He has seen lots of young, successful, people lose the plot. He was very worried about Rob. He had been out in Rob's company and saw Rob burning it at both ends.' Several years later Rob would describe the period as 'a pitiful year'. Comfort eating had led him to put on three stone. He was so hooked on drink and drugs that he could not face even those closest to him. Jan, terrified about what was happening to her son, would travel down from Stoke to London and bang on his door to be let in. Rob, too ashamed to see his mother in the state he was in, would ignore her. 'I didn't want to see her. I was off my face,' he remembers. 'When we eventually did meet up, it would be with me full of shame and tears. What had happened to her beautiful baby boy?' Other times he'd stay up all night partying, then dose himself up with sleeping pills washed down with four cans of Special Brew lager and get on the early train at 7 a.m. from London to Stoke. He'd arrive in his home town dishevelled, with his clothes torn and his shoes missing and crash out at Jan's for three or four days to recover. Then he would be back on a train to the capital to repeat the entire exercise

Kinsella was aware of the problem with Rob, but not how to solve it. He was also aware of Jan Williams's increasing antipathy towards him. As he had only ever planned to take on Williams in the short term, Kevin was now keen to off-load him to another manager, who could take his difficult client on to the next level. The situation between Kinsella, Rob and Jan would deteriorate very quickly and land Rob with a legal battle with the manager at the same time as he was in dispute on another front with his record company. As a one-time boxer, Kinsella was used to the pre-bout instruction to make it 'a good clean fight', but this was the music business where there's no such thing.

Rob's next choice of manager was greeted with as much head-scratching in the business as his appointment of Kevin Kinsella. Rob had met Tim Abbott during his infamous Glastonbury appearance in June 1995. Abbott, who pushed Williams on stage for his impromptu appearance with the Gallagher brothers, was a former marketing man at Alan McGee's Creation label, the record company Oasis were signed to. His claim to fame had, until this point, been to appear on the cover of the Oasis single "Cigarettes and Alcohol". The move to appoint him as his manager was odd, in that Abbott had never managed a major artist. He got the Robbie Williams job when Rob rang him after his split from Kevin Kinsella in December and told him: 'You got me into this mess, now get me out of it.' Rob had hit it off with Abbott immediately they met on the Oasis bus at the back of the main stage at the festival. Like his young new client, Abbott, then 38, was not adverse to a bit of the rock'n'roll lifestyle. He was well known and liked in the business. And because of Rob's obsession with all things Oasis at the time, he seemed the perfect choice. Like Kinsella, however, Abbott would soon learn he had been handed a poisoned chalice.

CHAPTER SIX
freedom

In the palatial surroundings of a beautifully appointed hotel suite in Cologne the party was in full swing. A group of stunning German girls, hand-picked for the occasion and dressed up to the nines, were mixing with Robbie Williams's entourage. Alcohol and drugs were in plentiful supply, but the host was nowhere to be seen. As usual, though, Rob had a spectacular entrance planned. High above the revellers, the singer, perched atop the suite's ornate minstrel's gallery, let out a deranged cackle and dropped his trousers.

Two hours earlier, in a drunken and paranoid state, the hotel's most demanding guest that night had embarked on the ultimate act of rock'n'roll rebellion and set about trashing his room. He had passed out before the damage and his bill for the repairs to smashed vases, antique furniture and two ripped sofas had reached £8,000. Now, awake again and ready to wreak some more havoc, Rob was all set for the evening's entertainment to begin. But his impromptu party piece spoilt the mood of his guests. The disgusted girls walked out and Rob was put to bed by his long-suffering aides. For good measure they locked him in his suite, but Rob was in no mood to have an early night. Naked and wrecked, he opened the French doors that led out of his suite and staggered outside on to the balcony, several storeys above the traffic below. Now clambering on top of the balcony in the cold air, he stood upright for a moment then lurched forward into space. A second later his foot found the top of the veranda to the neighbouring suite. Swaying backwards again, he found his balance and repeated the death-defying manoeuvre. Moments later he was banging on the window of manager Tim Abbott. The terrified Abbott rescued his client, but Rob was far from finished. Taking flight from his panicking colleague as he was led back to his room, the up-market guests were treated to the sight of their most famous fellow resident streaking through the corridors of the hotel with Abbott hot on his tail. As he gave his pursuer the slip once again, Rob was now pushing the button to call the lift. 'I want to find a photographer to take my picture,' he yelled. His manager swooped as the stark naked singer was stepping onto the lift down to the lobby. Rob passed out on the spot to be carried back to his room comatose.

The evening had started off innocently enough, Rob, in Cologne for a television appearance, turned down an invitation to join his team at a party being thrown in the city. He told his aides he was planning to stay in to see if he could chat up Spice Girl Mel B, who was staying with her band in the same hotel. Rob had not had success in tracking down Scary Spice. Instead, bad tempered and petulant at finding himself alone, he hit the bottle and then began his wrecking spree. Abbott returned to find Rob in tears. 'Why did you leave me? Why did you go out without me?' he wailed.

Kevin Kinsella had attempted to sign Rob to the hugely successful U2 manager, Paul McGuinness, but the Irishman had passed on the offer. Abbott was next in line. His task would be to extricate Rob from his RCA deal and sign him to a new label. There was no shortage of record companies willing to take him on. The likelihood would be, though, that Rob would have to be bought out of his deal with his old label before he could begin making records elsewhere. 1996 would start the way 1995 ended – with legal papers, court hearings and complex negotiations. The process of actually making any music was not on the horizon.

Heading the queue for his signature was EMI. The company's UK president JF Cecillion was a long-time admirer of Williams. As far as the Frenchman was concerned, the young man had 'star quality'. Also in the frame was London Records, home of Take That rivals East 17. Rob had met with executives from the label who were said to be preparing an offer to sign him. Meanwhile a court date of February 26 was set aside for the hearing to decide his dispute with RCA and its parent company BMG. In the phoney war that preceded the hearing, the talk from both sides was tough. Rob's people accused RCA of 'intransigence'. 'The money they want is too high,' said a Robbie aide. 'Robbie hasn't yet proved himself, but the stakes are very high.' Rob's case would be that RCA/BMG, in refusing to release him from his contract with them, were guilty of unreasonable restraint of trade. The stakes were, indeed, high. If Rob had gone to court and lost the case he could, very well, have seen the last of his £1 million nest egg from his Take That days. In the event, Rob would not have to take to the witness box. At the eleventh hour, the sides came to an out-of-court agreement. Rob was forced to issue a grovelling apology to his masters. The star said he was 'extremely sorry' to have brought the case and had to pay an estimated £250,000 in costs. 'I now fully accept the validity and enforceability of my BMG recording contract. I remain a BMG artist,' he said. His objection to the release of *Take That: Greatest Hits*, which was due out in March, was also withdrawn. The settlement was announced in a two-minute hearing. Rob was not in court.

For the time being, at least, Rob would be forced to remain on the books of the label. The situation was made doubly worse by the news announced a little under two weeks before Rob was due to step into court. On February 13, Rob's 22nd birthday, Take That called a press conference to announce the band was splitting after six years together. It was hardly a welcome present. Howard Donald and Jason Orange would take time out to think about what to do with their careers, Mark Owen and Gary Barlow would become solo singers. This left Rob in the position of being potentially one of three ex-Take That stars on the same label and with the certain knowledge that Gary would be the jewel in the crown of RCA's talent. Since Rob's departure, the clock had been ticking down on the final days of Take That. Now, with the band's demise, Gary could begin what many predicted would be an even bigger career without his boy band shackles. His record company would be, of course, Take That's label RCA. It was a nightmare scenario for Rob and his manager Tim Abbott. The history of pop was littered with former members of teen bands who had taken Route One to obscurity. The name of former Wham! heart-throb Andrew Ridgeley was enough to strike terror into the heart of any boy-band exile.

Despite the setback, Rob couldn't resist a final bit of fun at the expense of his old pals. After the announcement by the band that they had split and would not perform together again, Rob made them an offer they felt they had every right to refuse. In a statement, issued to the Press rather than the band themselves, Rob offered to re-form the group for one final concert as a goodbye to the fans. 'I know we've had our differences, but one thing keeps coming back to haunt me – simply that Take That have not given their fans the farewell they want and deserve,' he said. Rob's offer was to re-form the group at a UK stadium such as Wembley or Old Trafford and play a final gig. His only stipulation would be that all profits, including from merchandising, would go to charity. 'I never had the chance to say goodbye to our fans and it's something that will always stick in my throat. Now that you have all gone your separate ways, I guarantee you'll all soon feel the same way. It's the fans who made Take That and gave us our success. They are owed a proper goodbye from ALL of us. They deserve to see Take That perform live one last time. Come on, boys, let's do it.' Rob told his ex co-stars.

There can surely have been little doubt in Rob's mind what reaction he would get from his former cohorts. When Nigel Martin-Smith heard of the 'offer' he went ballistic. In a withering attack on Rob, he issued a statement dismissing any chance of a reunion. Branding Rob's approach 'a cheap trick', he said the four remaining Take That members had been silent since Rob's departure. 'Unlike Robbie they have not used the Press to reply to his comments or vent their frustrations and anger at his many outbursts. Take That ended their career in a dignified manner and they have no wish to enter into a Press battle about an event that will never happen and with a person who has not bothered to contact them personally. It's terrible that the fans are still having their hopes raised in this cruel way,' he said.

Despite the court settlement, Rob was in no mood to let bygones be bygones. As the deal was announced he spoke of his 'betrayal' by his one-time friends. And, despite admitting crying himself to sleep at nights since leaving the group, he was bullish. 'There were five minutes on Christmas Day when I saw them on telly and thought, "I wish I was up there' – but only because I know I would have done it better,' he sneered.

As the ink dried on the out-of-court deal and the lawyers prepared their bills, Rob was heading for the sun. His companion for his trip to Barbados was the Honourable Jacqueline Hamilton-Smith, the 28-year-old daughter of Lord Colwyn. Rob flew to Barbados on Concorde to stay at a villa owned by the make-up artist's father. She met him as he landed at the airport and the couple put on a steamy show, French-kissing and 'almost undressing each other' for embarrassed passengers and less embarrassed members of the Press. Rob said he was looking forward to a complete rest, 'I really need it,' he said. The remainder of the trip was conducted mainly in front of, and occasionally for, the cameras. Rob in knee-length checked shorts, frolicking in the waves with bikini-girl Jacqui, who looked great. Rob didn't. If they made pies in Barbados it's safe to say they would have had a run on them during the Williams visit. Like a tartan beach ball, sporting a bad hair-do, Rob certainly had the look of someone about to be released from a record contract. He didn't, however, have the look of someone who was ever likely to get another one. The six months on the sofa were apparent to all. Rob, who admitted living off beer and cheese-and-onion crisps, made little attempt to hide his bulging waistline. He was probably aware of the futility of such a cover-up. Without the letters and warnings from Nigel Martin-Smith about his weight, Rob looked like a child who had been let loose in the er...pie shop.

The unlikely couple had met at a showbiz party thrown by producer Nellee Hooper, who earlier had warned Kevin Kinsella about his fears for Rob's health. Jacqui was also a close friend of actress Patsy Kensit. The previous November the pair met again in Manchester and shared a night out with Patsy and Rob's new pal Liam Gallagher. The evening would end with both wild-men finding love. Jacqui, who lived in a £500,000 house in Maida Vale, west London, was credited with getting Rob out of tracksuits and woolly hats and into pinstripe suits. He, in turn, was said to be so smitten with the convent-educated beauty that he had taken her home to Stoke to introduce her to his beloved grandmother, Betty. The 83-year-old had no idea who the posh girl was and asked her, 'What's your name, duck?' Betty was mortified when she read in the papers that her grandson's new girlfriend was aristocracy. 'I nearly had a fit. I felt so embarrassed that I called her duck,' she said. When Jacqui's mother, Sonia, Lady Colwyn, was first told by her daughter that she was dating the singer, she had to ask the landlady of her local pub in the Cotswold village of Gretton if she'd heard of him. 'I gather he's some sort of pop star, apparently,' said her ladyship. Lady Sonia was introduced to her daughter's new boyfriend at the funeral of Jacqui's grandmother, Lady Miriam Colwyn. He was invited to spend the weekend at her mother's country home, Witch House, where she lives with Jacqui's stepfather John Underwood. But Lady Colwyn had seemed less than taken with her daughter's new man. Asked if she thought he would be her new son-in-law, she was said to have exclaimed: 'I really don't think he would be suitable.' Jacqui's father, Lord Colwyn, an eminent Harley Street dental surgeon, was also nonplussed by the relationship. He was inundated with calls to his office from teenagers asking for a home number for Robbie.

There was little cheer to be had on Rob's arrival back in the UK. RCA announced that the first Robbie Williams single would not be released until both Gary Barlow and Mark Owen had released their first post-Take That offerings. Rob's manager Tim Abbott complained: 'Robbie's very upset. He feels patronized, not prioritized.' Behind the scenes, though, there was feverish activity. At least five record companies were vying for the Robbie Williams signature, including London Record, Parlophone, EMI, Mercury and Virgin.

By late June, a couple of weeks short of a year after leaving Take That, Rob's nightmare appeared to be coming to an end. RCA agreed to let him leave the company and he signed a £1.5-million deal with formerly defunct EMI offshoot, Chrysalis. In addition, EMI would pay £800,000 to RCA to buy Rob out his contract with them. The new deal would leave the way open for him to do battle with arch-rival Gary Barlow, whose first solo single with RCA, "Forever Love", would be released on July 8. Rob's attack on the charts would kick off on the 29th. While Gary's single was a self-penned effort, Rob, although busy writing poetry, was having problems with the music. Desperate to get a record out as soon as possible, it was EMI president JF Cecillion's idea to release a cover version of George Michael's hit "Freedom". The lyrics and sentiments of the record were clearly apt for a singer released from firstly his boy-band prison and secondly his record-company contract. But the choice of single begged an important question: if Robbie Williams wanted to be taken seriously as a singer and songwriter, if he wanted more than just singing along to the words Gary Barlow had written, what the hell had he been doing for the last 12 months? The sceptics included George Michael, who was initially less than enthusiastic about Rob releasing his song. The evening before giving a Press conference to announce the single, Rob had called up his new friend to tell him he was planning to put out the single. The ex-Wham! star was unconvinced, but he relented when Rob sent him a copy of the video for the record. In the event, the Williams version, unsurprisingly entitled "Freedom '96" was a barely passable attempt at the song. It also failed to give any clue as to whether, once the Take That gloss had worn off the singer, he would have anything to offer beyond a predictably short solo career. While Gary had scored a number one hit with "Forever Love", Rob had to make do with number two. Always good for a dig at his old colleague, Rob proclaimed, 'I don't like "Forever Love". I know Gary's talented and he's got many brilliant songs. I just don't understand that track.' But Rob was also unhappy with his own single. He desperately wanted to carve out a new niche for himself and "Freedom '96" had not helped in his quest. The problem for those around him was that Rob didn't really know what exactly he wanted to do with his career. Not being a musician, his problem was obvious. While he had scores of ideas for lyrics, there were no tunes to go with them. Executives from EMI, sensing their £1 million plus investment was looking, to say the least, shaky, decided to sit their newest star down with a writing partner with a formidable reputation for producing hits.

Again, the decision to fly Rob and EMI A&R man Chris Briggs down to Miami to work with hit-maker Desmond Child was Cecillion's. The exercise was less than successful. The pair produced Rob's next single, "Old Before I Die", but the combination of the write-to-order Child, who had penned many of the hits for permed rockers Bon Jovi, and Williams was disastrous. Rob was so miserable in the Miami sunshine he told Briggs he was going back to London early. He had nothing in common with Child, the hit-making machine who churned out songs on his Florida conveyor belt. Rob was looking for someone he could connect with, who felt the same way he did, who got his gags. The final straw for Rob had been when they finished recording the track and were cooling off in the pool in the grounds of the American's Miami mansion. 'Do you like the house?' asked

Child. 'You helped pay for it.' Label head Cecillion threat-ened to fly out to the States to sort out the problem and Rob agreed to stay, but he eventually flew back to the UK still looking for the right musical partnership.

Robbie's behaviour in Cologne was enough to persuade Abbott of the sheer scale of Rob's problems with drink and drugs. He decided his client should be sent out of the UK to keep him away from the temptations on offer in London. He believed he could clean Rob up if he was kept out of the media spotlight. The plan was scuppered by Cecillion, who wanted his man in Britain. Meanwhile, those who knew the couple were aware that Rob's relationship with Jacqui Hamilton-Smith was not doing him much good either. Long credited as a having a stabilizing effect on him, Jacqui herself had a taste for alcohol and partying that almost rivalled her boyfriend's. Pete was convinced Jacqui was not helping his son and Abbott complained that the pair would lie in bed till lunchtime then emerge for marathon drinking sessions. Rob told his incredulous manager he had been lying in bed with his aristocratic girlfriend the previous night and she had asked how many times he had been in love. He told her there had been lots of girls, but he had probably been in love only three or four times. When he asked the Honourable Jacqueline how many times she had given her heart, he was in for a shock. 'Forty-three,' she replied.

In his pitiful state, Rob began suffering terrifying halluci-nations. At the house he shared with Jacqui he began feeling the presence of spirits. He would think tape decks had spon-taneously begun to play music and would hear the locks turning in the front door. Eventually, the spirits he thought he could hear on the stairs were running around the end of his bed. Whenever he went out he felt they were following him. It got so bad he would take a bottle of vodka to bed with him and mix it with sleeping tablets just to get some respite from the 'demons'. In the end he had to move out of the house and into the Swiss Cottage Marriott Hotel. His fear was multiplied when he discovered the area had been a Black Death burial site. Rob's experience of the paranormal went back to his childhood in the Red Lion. Once, as Pete was taking the young Rob past the closed bar, the youngster pointed in and asked Pete what those two men were still doing in there. Pete, knowing no one was there, told Rob they were just drinking. His son began to look frightened, so Pete told Rob to wave goodbye to them. 'Dad, they haven't got any hands,' Rob told his spooked father.

Problems for an ailing Rob were compounded by a new legal wrangle. On August 6, 1996, Nigel Martin-Smith came back to haunt him. He issued a writ at the High Court in London claiming damages against his ex-client. Martin-Smith claimed the singer owed him £31,881.30 from a £135,000 royalty cheque Williams had received from his time with Take That. He also claimed another £47,000 from a £200,000 advance that had been paid to Rob for *Take That: Greatest Hits*. If that wasn't bad enough, Martin-Smith also claimed he was owed 20 per cent of his discovery's earnings until 2001 and ten per cent after that until 2006. At a 'freedom party' two months earlier, where Rob celebrated the ending of his links with Take That and the scrapping of his RCA deal, he had told guests he wanted to run over Martin-Smith with a fork-lift truck. Now he must have wished he had carried through his idle threat. Not only was he faced with the damages claim, but if he was forced to fight the writ in court, the whole case could set him back £1 million.

Rob, while getting a reputation as the biggest ligger in showbusiness, was also becoming increasingly vocal in his attacks on Martin-Smith and his former Take That band mates. In an interview with gay magazine *Attitude*, he described Martin-Smith as 'a cunt' and Gary Barlow as a 'clueless wanker'. The rest of the band didn't fair much better. Only Mark Owen escaped his wrath. The others were, declared Rob, 'selfish, stupid, greedy, arrogant and thick'. Howard Donald remembers the band differently. 'Robbie says being in the band was like prison, but I have hours of camcorder tapes proving what a great time we had. We all had our fun and so did he,' he says.

CHAPTER SEVEN
showbiz samaritan

It's the most dreaded phone call in showbusiness. If Elton John rings out of the blue to see how you are, it generally means one of three things has happened: your career has gone down the toilet, your life has gone down the toilet or your career *and* your life have gone down the toilet. Like a latter-day Dr Barnardo for the famous, Elton collects showbiz waifs and strays, the fallen and the lost, ministering to them, tending and healing. You can imagine him and his partner, David Furnish, in Versace bathrobes and cashmere mules, scouring the morning papers for more celebrity misfortune, a new star to be offered succour and salvation. Then, as if things aren't bad enough, along comes the invitation round to Elton's £15-million mansion in Windsor or his pink palace on the Côte d'Azur.

OK, so only the terminally cynical and jaundiced would accuse that angel of mercy Elton of indulging in bouts of celebrity *schadenfreude*. Those who know him say he is humanitarian, comforting and nurturing his flock. Just ask Stephen Gately. The former Boyzone star's career hit the skids after he admitted he was gay. His record label dumped him and, in 2002, so did his boyfriend. Cue the call from Elton, a guided tour of the mansion follows and an offer to sing at one of his charity shows. The next thing he knows, Stephen's life is back on track and he lands the title role in the stage musical *Joseph and his Amazing Technicolour Dreamcoat*. Elton was also there for serial bad boy Robert Downey Jnr when he was jailed for drug offences. He took the troubled star under his wing and even let him stand in for him on the video for his song "I Want Love".

So it was no surprise when Rob received word that the Samaritan to the stars had heard of his plight and wanted to help. In fact, not only had Elton heard of Rob's troubles, he had seen them at first hand. Rob had got so blind drunk at a party thrown by Elton at his Berkshire home earlier that year that he threw up in front of embarrassed guests. Elton became concerned about his young guest. In the late summer of 1996, Rob was at a low ebb, drunk and depressed, he had reached the point where he was no longer communicating with those around him. His parents had begun to have their first real fears that he might try to harm himself, but even Jan, so long Rob's rock, could not get her son to talk to her about his problems. Elton was also acutely aware of the signs. In the early 1970s he had taken on a punishing schedule of touring and recording that left him exhausted and depressed. His decline saw him hit the bottle and begin a battle with drugs. At his lowest point he had considered suicide. Now clean and rejuvenated, Elton was keen to pass on his experiences and advice to a young man with whom he saw many parallels.

Jan had retrained as a drink and drugs counsellor after having abandoning her florist business. Even so, she was grateful for Elton's intervention. Since the previous Christmas she had been at her wits' end over her son's descent into a black hole of his own making. She had witnessed a change in his personality. Rob, says Jan, had always been a very polite child. 'He was the sort of kid who always said "thank you" whether it was for a meal or just a lift somewhere. But he stopped doing that and he'd use any excuse not to stay long. He seemed to find it uncomfortable and difficult.' Take That, she says, had taken away her boy's 'innocence'. 'He went in as a child and came out a man.' Rob had been stifled and browbeaten by the experience. Denied the chance to voice an opinion he was told to 'keep his mouth shut' in interviews and not to take the limelight away from Gary Barlow, Jan believed. Jan knew her son was in denial for a long time. 'You can't treat somebody for drink and drugs problems until they've addressed the issues for themselves,' she added. It was at that point that 'he admitted what the rest of us knew and was able to get help.'

The whole thing resembled a scene from *Trainspotting*. Rob woke as usual in the middle of the afternoon. It took him a moment to work out where he was. He was alone in his London home except for his two goldfish Vodka and Tonic. The place was a mess. Next to him was a bowl over-flowing with cigarette butts stacked on top of long-forgotten cornflakes. His bed sheets hadn't been changed for weeks. Empty bottles of vodka were strewn over the bedroom floor. Rob staggered out of bed. Bloated and ugly, he had for a long time been unable to face himself in the mirror. He was desperate for a drink, but also frightened. He reached for a bottle, but instead of pouring a drink, he sat down and picked up the phone.

Rob got an answerphone. His message was desperate. He was scared and needed help. Within half an hour Elton, on tour in America, was ringing Rob back. The message had scared him as well. Fearing for his friend, he told Rob to get his stuff together and go to his house in Windsor immediately. Rob remained at Elton's house for two weeks being cared for by the superstar's staff. The stay put him back together enough to return home. When Elton returned from America, Rob visited the singer to thank him for helping him and broke down in tears and admitted his addiction problems to his friend.

For a long time, Elton had been trying to get Rob to face the fact that he was getting into serious trouble. Ever since Rob's drunken antics at Elton's party in the summer, he had kept in touch with the young singer, concerned he was losing control. Now, with Rob's admission that he needed help, Elton was able to begin the process of getting him back on track and suggested he visit Irish therapist Beechy Colclough. In September, following the release of "Freedom '96", Rob began to see the drink and drugs therapist who has two Charter Nightingale Clinics in London. Colclough was already famous as the man Elton credited with saving his life for helping him beat his addiction to cocaine and drink. Over a period of years he had become known as the therapist to the stars. He had treated Michael Jackson for his addiction to painkillers and his latest famous client was England footballer Paul Gascoigne, whom

Colclough was trying to wean off the bottle. Twice a week, Rob had one-to-one sessions with the 49-year-old therapist, who had become a famous face thanks to his advice slot on GMTV. Along with his addiction to alcohol and cocaine, Rob's increasing reliance on slimming pills was worrying the people closest to him. The sessions were emotional with the singer pouring out his heart over the disastrous turn his life had taken. The final straw had been a three-day bender during which Rob had been on a booze cruise around the capital's most happening night spots. The non-stop drinking session had started on Friday night and ended with Rob comatose on a friend's floor on Sunday. Elton had seen the frightening similarities with his own descent into addiction. He identified with the binges that went on for days and ended in passing out in a heap. For Rob, it had taken the intervention of a star he had revered since he was a child to make him acknowledge his many problems and finally submit to treatment. For Colclough's part his analysis was straightforward. 'Addictive personalities can be rich or poor. Stars don't have more problems except when they are found comatose in the street and plastered all over the newspapers,' he said.

Jan was relieved that her son was addressing his problems. She said at the time, 'It's lucky Rob faced up to it so quickly. Some people spend years and years in denial.' The last 12 months had been the worst of his mother's life. But, by the autumn, Jan was hopeful Rob might be able to beat his addiction problems, having faced up to the fact he needed help and accepted Elton's offer of assistance. Elton took Rob on a shopping spree in London's Bond Street. In Elton's favourite jewellers, Theo Fennell, Rob spotted a diamond-encrusted cross. When they got back to Elton's house, he handed Rob a box with the cross inside. Rob said of Elton, 'To some people he is just a strange man in a red PVC Versace suit. To me, he's an angel.' Jan saw a change in Rob. At the time she said, 'Robert is in better health now and happier than he has been for a long time. He is more like the son I knew before he went into Take That six years ago.' He was healthy again and had even taken up golf, joining his mum on the course for a round when he went home. But, despite the upbeat assessment, Jan let slip the problem that Rob and those around him still faced. 'He rarely drinks and does not take drugs. Considering all he has gone through he is absolutely fantastic,' she said. But it was the word 'rarely' that was memorable. Despite the help of Elton and his sessions with Beechy Colclough, Rob was, it had to be said, still drinking. And although it was unspoken between them, all those in Rob's life knew he would not be out of the woods until Jan was able to substitute the word 'rarely' for 'never'.

As if Rob didn't have enough problems he was about to add another manager to the list of those already suing him. Ever since his split from Kevin Kinsella, the two men had been in dispute about how much money Kinsella was owed by Rob. Rob's lawyers had denied there had ever been a formal agreement between the two men, but Kinsella was seeking £400,000 in unpaid bills and costs. The case brought against Rob by Nigel Martin-Smith was on-going and now Tim Abbott was about to become the third manager to call in the lawyers. Word that Rob had sacked Abbott came as news leaked out about his visits to Colclough. The timing could not have been worse. Rob, it seemed to the world, was up to his eyes in it on every front. He had announced his split with Abbott and his company Proper Management at the end of October 1996, but insisted the situation between him and his now ex-manager remained amicable. Rob said he felt it was time 'to move on' and cited that old chestnut, a desire for 'artistic freedom', as the reason for the two going their separate ways. 'Tim's been a fantastic help to me over the past months. We had great success with the single "Freedom". We haven't fallen out and I know we'll continue to be friends,' he said. But someone should have told Abbott, because he was in no mood to wave a fond farewell to his most difficult client.

On the very day Rob was playing down any friction between the two, Abbott was preparing to call in the lawyers. He was furious that he had been shown the door by Rob and vowed to sue him over more unpaid fees. An angry Abbott said: 'We are extremely disappointed that, despite all our efforts over the past year and the tremendous change in Rob's career we have achieved, he should choose to bring our relationship to an end at such a crucial stage. I would like to think we could settle the problem of my claim without litigation but I am afraid that it seems inevitable that Rob's lawyers will shortly be hearing from mine. And it seems the whole matter will become subject to the jurisdiction of the courts.' Abbott certainly had a strong case. He had negotiated the deal to free Rob from his contract with RCA and signed him to EMI in a lucrative piece of business. His announcement that he would be becoming the third former aide to issue proceedings was almost unprecedented, even in the notoriously litigious world of pop music.

Rob appeared to be trapped in a pincer movement. On the personal front his life, too, he was also under the cosh. As he headed into treatment, he headed out of his relationship with Jacqui Hamilton-Smith. The couple said they remained friends and she was said to be 'delighted' that Rob had sought help for his problems. Rob denied the split had come as a result of newspaper claims that he had dated actress Sally Anne Marsh, star of X-rated West End show *Voyeurz*. Just a month before they broke up, Rob had issued a mission statement for his life. In upbeat mode he said, 'I'm bored with being pissed. I'm bored with being fat and I'm really bored with being depressed. I want to be thin. I like looking good and I know I looked a mess. People see me going out and getting drunk, but I've been really depressed. It feels good to be Robbie again because for so long I hated myself.'

The optimism, though, was looking decidedly premature. In the wake of his split from Jacqui, Rob was back out on the tiles again. His nights out with the lads, often including members of Blur, were already becoming legendary and he was a regular sight in Soho drinking den the Groucho Club, playing snooker with actor Keith Allen and continually missing his turn because of rather too many visits to the toilets. Rob had described his relationship with Jacqui as being 'in the mire'. She moved out of the Maida Vale home she had been sharing with Rob and back into her mother's house in Chelsea. 'Our problems are partly down to work,' said Rob. Work was certainly a problem, Rob was writing and working on demos in the studio, but in all honesty, most were, at best, second rate. The release date of his next single "Old Before I Die" had been put back and he was in desperate need of focus. Without a manager, he needed a saviour.

CHAPTER EIGHT
saviours

There are occasions when you just get lucky. Something comes along when you least expect it and, bam! – a new door opens, new horizons, a new path. It's safe to say that in the dying days of 1996, if Rob had remained consistent in his choice of advisors he would now be just another show-business footnote, a '20 things you didn't know about boy band failures' tabloid feature, a relic succumbing to the humiliation of *Celebrity Big Brother* and *I'm a Celebrity Get Me Out Of Here* oblivion. The split from Abbott found him staring into the abyss. With his career and personal life at a crossroads, the signs weren't hopeful.

The Abbott period shuddered to a close with his manager finding it increasingly difficult to communicate with the troubled singer. Abbott had taken to ringing Jan to complain about the erratic behaviour of her son. Jan, sick of the aggravation, told Tim to pull out, to call it a day with Rob if it wasn't working out between the two of them. Rob had also tired of the relationship. At first, Abbott had the gloss of being part of the Oasis set, the credibility that, as far as

Williams was concerned, infected everything and anybody who came near the Manchester rockers. Abbott was up for a good time, as 'mad for it' as the rest, but the relationship had soured. Abbott became weary of the constant hand-holding, the moods, the belligerence, his client's endless demands and drug-induced paranoia. When the pair had made a trip to France, Abbott decided they would go on the Eurostar. With childlike enthusiasm, Rob became animated at the prospect of his first trip on the cross-channel train. When the day of the trip arrived and they headed for the first-class carriage, Abbott noticed Rob had left his luggage on the concourse. He had become so used to having flunkeys to cater for his every need during his Take That days that he had never actually carried his own bags. Abbott told him to go back and collect them himself.

Rob's finances were also in such a perilous state that his credit cards were perennially refused. This did not, however, put him off one of his favourite hobbies – shopping. Abbott would be frequently called upon to pay for everything from *Star Wars* memorabilia in New York, to mammoth clothes-buying sessions, food and, of course, drink. He would also, he insisted privately, have to shell out for anti-bugging equipment from security shops, as Rob became more and more paranoid that he was being eavesdropped on. The Oasis connection, which had been the reason the two men had got together in the first place, had also become a source of embarrassment. The Gallagher brothers had noticeably cooled in their attitude to Rob, putting Abbott in an unenviable position. While in New York to see Oasis at Madison Square Gardens, Rob and Abbott had watched the show, but when he tried to see his new 'friends' backstage, Rob discovered that only his manager had been left a backstage pass by the brothers. He and Abbott now began a long and predictable battle in the courts that would see another large chunk of Rob's fortune end up in the pockets of lawyers.

Rob and Jan sought the help of his accountant Richard Harvey as he began the search for the fourth manager of his relatively short career. Harvey was a trusted member of the Williams team and had the added benefit of a long career working in and around the music business. He compiled a list of people he thought could work with Rob, the sort of figures who could handle an artist whose many and varied problems were obvious even on the most cursory of inspections. One of the companies Rob was put in touch with was IE Music, run by Tim Clark and David Enthoven. The two men, already well into middle age, were a couple of dinosaurs of the music business who had been round the block more times that they cared to remember. In a world increasingly occupied by corporate suits, they were unashamedly of a different time, pioneers from the hippie era who, despite outward appearances, were shrewd and respected operators.

The pair had known each other for years. Clark, who had originally been involved in marketing ska bands in the 1960s, had joined Island Records. Enthoven, a plummy-voiced Old Harrovian, had begun his involvement in the business as a roadie before taking on the job of manager to a series of small bands. He was managing prog rock outfit King Crimson when he met Clark, who was responsible for signing the band to Island. David's company EG took on Roxy Music and later the solo Bryan Ferry and T Rex. But the 1980s saw a change in fortunes for the two men. While Clarke continued his association with Island, Enthoven was busy flushing his life down the pan. His company had become highly successful, allowing him to blow large amounts of cash on a lavish lifestyle that included more than 40 motorbikes. But a more dangerous hobby was putting a fortune's worth of coke up his nose and graduating to a full-on heroin addiction. By 1977 he was about to see everything he had built go up in smoke. His partners dumped him because of his drugged-up state, his marriage collapsed and he lost touch with his children. The bike collection had to be sold and he lost his home. By the mid-1980s he was living in squalor in his late mother's house, sleeping in her bed with his two dogs. He seriously considered suicide, but was persuaded to go into rehab by an old friend. Enthoven emerged clean, but broke, and moved into a bedsit while he began trying to rebuild his wrecked life. He touted for work and slowly began building up his management business with small bands. In 1991 he met up with Tim Clark again and they set up IE Music. The pair renewed their relationship with Bryan Ferry before being asked to work with Massive Attack. In late 1996, accountant Richard Harvey, who had links to Ferry, put the team in touch with a former boy band singer who desperately needed a leg-up.

When Rob walked into Clark and Enthoven's west London offices he was not a pretty sight. Neither man knew what to expect or, indeed, were that familiar with his career so far. What they realised immediately was that here was a young man with a lot of problems. Enthoven describes the Rob he met that day as being 'like a caged animal'. But shining through the obvious trouble was the desire and hunger to carry on entertaining people, to be making records, to be up on stage. Their next encounter with Rob came as Tim and David sat in the audience of the MTV awards. Rob, hosting the show, had impressed them with his presence and coolness in a role where many have come unstuck. The two men were invited to Rob's house to listen to some of his demos. They were underwhelmed. The music he played them was at best average. Perhaps sensing their lack of enthusiasm for his musical efforts, Rob changed tack. 'Do you want to hear some of my poetry?' he asked.

What the music had lacked, the words Rob read to the two men made up for in spades. They were heartfelt, funny and raw. Clark and Enthoven knew the kid had talent, the question was – what to do with it? It was obvious that a musician needed to be brought in, someone who could take Rob's obvious wordsmith potential and put it to music. The process was at first hit and miss. Rob was still in a bad way. The progress he had made with Beechy Colclough had proved to be a false dawn. He was drinking again, in huge quantities. He used coke to stay awake long enough to drink more. His state of mind, therefore, was not exactly conducive to forging a relationship with a new writing partner. The early attempts ended in failure and still nothing to give EMI in terms of the album for which the pop world and, more importantly, his fans had been waiting 18 months. Salvation came in the shape of Liverpool-raised Guy Chambers, who, at 34, had been around the music scene for a while. Chambers came from a musical family. His father was a flautist with the London Philharmonic and his mother had worked at record label Decca. Guy started playing guitar in bands as a teenager. At 15, the group he was then in, Hambi and the Dance, was signed by Virgin. The band didn't have much success and Guy set off to London to do a music degree. After music school he drifted around playing piano in the bars of London and living from hand to mouth. He was taken off the dole with an offer to play keyboards for Liverpool band The Teardrop Explodes. He went on to fill the same role in two other bands, the Waterboys and Karl Wallinger's World Party.

But it was Guy's ambition to front his own band and he formed the Lemon Trees, playing guitar and singing. They didn't exactly set the world on fire, although Rob's mum Jan had been a fan. The truth was Guy had neither the looks nor vocal ability to afford the group anything other than fringe status. The word, however, was out that Rob had a new management team and they were looking for a composer to hook up with their poetry-writing former teen idol. If David Enthoven had any hair he would have been pulling it out. He and Clark had been wading through scores of demo tapes, looking for the elusive writing partner for their new client. By chance, a friend of Guy's had recommended that he submit a tape to the pair. Clark and Enthoven had been given advance warning from contacts in the business that Chambers's demo would be worth a listen. His stuff stood out and a meeting between the two talents was arranged.

Rob likes a bit of mysticism: the runes, forces beyond our control, all that stuff. He is convinced the hand of a higher power was at work in bringing him together with the writing partner who would help him shift more than 20 million records in the next five years. He tells the story that his managers handed him a list of potential collaborators. He had no idea who Guy Chambers was and hadn't heard his music, but without hesitation he pointed to his name on the sheet of paper and said, 'That's him.'

Guy was not so sure. He knew enough about Robbie Williams to know he was a drugged-up, pissed-up wreck, who had been photographed across much of Greater London getting completely slaughtered. For Chambers, the serious musician, who wrote his first string quartet at the age of 12, the prospect of getting involved with a boy-band reject was dubious to say the least. But Clark and Enthoven were hopeful that the marrying of the two disciplines could produce something special. In Rob, they had a writer not afraid of exposing his feelings. He was capable of expressing anger, pain and love in equal measure. The words flowed out of him unchecked and instinctively. In Chambers they had spotted a musical magpie. Brought up listening to his mother's vast record collection, he had been drenched in a huge array of musical styles. The question was, would the combination work and would they get on?

Rob was introduced to Guy. The plan was for the two to sit down together and see if they could come up with any ideas. The next 48 hours, locked away in Guy's house, would, Rob says, save his life.

The combination was explosive. Within half an hour of that first meeting on January 8, 1997, the two had completed "South of the Border", which went on to become a single. They wrote three songs in one afternoon, "Killing Me", "Teenage Millionaire" and "Life Thru a Lens". The first tune

Guy played Rob was "Lazy Days". Rob liked it, but wanted to change the lyrics. By day two, the process had gone into overdrive. That day, January 9, the two took 20 minutes to write "Angels", the song that would change the world's perception of Rob forever. Guy remembers having 'flu and feeling rough. Rob says Guy got a migraine after finishing the song. 'I don't think it was a migraine,' Rob would later say. 'I think he made himself ill with excitement.' The two knew they were producing something special together. Clark and Enthoven wanted to know how things were going. Chambers played them the material they had written in those first heady two days. The management team couldn't believe it – they'd cracked it.

Rob was driven to Guy's house that morning in a taxi. The driver, recognizing the former Take That star, asked him what he was doing these days. Rob told him he had just started working with a new writing partner and they were coming up with some ideas to see if they would work for an album. That evening, clutching a tape of the newly finished "Angels", he told the same driver to stick it in the tape deck. 'That's a number one', said the cabbie. When Rob sang the song to his dad Pete in the car one day on the way to Nantwich, Pete made him sing it again. 'Every time he finished it I told him to start again and he would sing it all the way through. He sang it eight times in all. I wanted to remember how it went because it was so good,' Pete says. 'I kept singing it back to him so I would keep it in my head until I got to listen to the record. The next day, the tune was gone and it drove me mad trying to remember it.'

Job done. Break out the Monte Cristo's, light up, and, to

steal a line from Rob, 'sit back and watch the royalties stack up'. It should have been that simple, but like everything on Planet Williams it almost never is. Clark and Enthoven knew their boy had a batch of songs that were undoubtedly good enough to put him right back in the game. The new tunes that had spontaneously combusted in Guy's home studio placed Rob exactly where he needed to be. The plastic pop of Take That had been left in the past. The new songs with references to 'Cocaine Katy' were distinctly more adult. EMI was less sure about the direction, though. Its marketing department felt Rob needed to aim his music at his Take That fans. Building a new fan base would be difficult. He should concentrate on hanging on to the people who had put him where he was. Where he was, though, was not a good place to be. Not only was he hooked on alcohol and cocaine, he had also developed an addiction to prescription drugs for his depression. His nadir came when he finally succumbed to heroin. It made him sick and the experience left him terrified. He had run out of coke and tried heroin as a substitute. 'It was the worst experience of my life and I can say, hand on heart, that I will never do it again,' he said.

By March, Rob had lost weight ready for the release of "Old Before I Die", the track he had written with Desmond Child in Miami. The single should have hit the shops in January, but neither Rob nor his new managers were happy with it. They asked Guy Chambers to see what he thought of the record. He suggested they re-do it in London. This, though, had to be kept from the head of the label. A fortune had been spent on sending Rob to Florida, not only to write the song with Child, but also to record it there. The re-working of the track had put back the release date and EMI were screaming for a new single.

Rob looked more like a pop star, but he still felt like a drunk. In public, he was upbeat, thanking Elton John for helping him sort out his life. Beechy Colclough, he said, had helped him 'unravel a few things about myself. He made me realize that I really don't want to be the George Best of pop.' But his problems with addictions were far from solved. While promoting "Old Before I Die" Rob admitted he was still drinking. 'I'm not totally reformed,' he said. 'I still drink, but recently I was able to pull back before I got completely out of it. I'm not proud of saying that, but I want to be honest.' And he admitted that Elton would hit the roof over his admission. 'I wish I could kick it completely, but I haven't yet,' he said. "Old Before I Die" failed to make the top spot in the charts, peaking at number two. The song, a clever enough take on Pete Townshend's 'Hope I die before I get old' refrain in "My Generation", was a sub-Oasis guitar-driven rocker, catchy, but a musical wax-work. Rob, always a good mimic since his debut at the Red Lion in Burslem, did his best Liam, paying homage to his idol from Burnage. The key change for the final chorus proved that at least Rob's voice was up to belting them out with the best of them. But essentially the record was little more than an imitation, a *Stars in their Eyes* phono-fit: 'Tonight, Matthew, I'm going to be Liam Gallagher of Oasis'. It offered no real idea of who the new, improved Robbie Williams, of the marketing campaigns and PR blitz, really was. Worse, it would inspire Noel Gallagher's later taunts that Rob was nothing more than 'a fat karaoke singer'. There was enough of the Take That momentum to guarantee a hit for the single, but there were already signs that it would be only a matter of time before Rob would be judged solely by the standards of what he was producing here and now and could not rely on the fans of his former band to bail out his next chart attempt. The new stuff he had written with Guy Chambers would need to do the business.

The process of writing the new songs would be a breeze compared to the business of actually getting them down on tape. Recording can be an arduous and demanding proposition at the best of times. It can be all the more difficult when your singer and lyricist is lying under the mixing desk in the foetal position clutching a bottle of Chateauneuf du Pape. Robbie Williams has always been a reluctant recording artist. He likes to see the whites of audience's eyes. For him, singing has always been about getting a reaction from the listener: feedback and love. He has never got on with standing in front of a microphone in a sound-proof booth, watching a few technicians pushing faders up and down, twiddling knobs and paying absolutely no attention whatsoever to his performance. In later, sober years, Rob would take to standing naked except for headphones and a fag while he laid down his vocal tracks. Now, he made do with any substance, legal or not, to distract him from the rigours of the job in hand. There were days when Chambers and his co-producer Steve Power got nothing out of their reluctant artist. Nothing, at least, that didn't sound like the nocturnal, patriotic wailings of a whisky-soaked drunk between bar and chip shop.

The boom or bust approach to his weight, which has been a perennial issue for the singer, was also evident. Once the promos, photo shoots and interviews were finished, once the *Top of the Pops* and TV had been recorded, Rob was off the leash again, back on the chocolate, the take-aways and the chips. He was also back on the town – not that he had ever really stopped.

How much is enough? At what point does everything pull in sharp focus? What does it take for the cartoon light bulb above your head to flicker into life? That moment of clarity for Rob didn't come with a long hard look in the mirror. He had been shying away from that particular confrontation for months. Perhaps, as an avid reader of his own publicity, it came when he studied the pictures of himself emerging at 3 a.m. from London's Hanover Grand nightclub. He was with a blonde, who wasn't his new girlfriend, the actress Anna Friel. This was a girl he met in the club, but, anyway, she wasn't really the problem. The real problem was all there in that series of frames, fired off by the paparazzi between club entrance and taxi. Those few snatched images said more than the tearful pleading from his mum, the warnings from his friend Elton John and the 'take it easy' advice from his worried managers. Caught in the stark light of a flash bulb, there below the Ryman's sign, the toll of the last two years was evident, even to the eyes of a self-deluded alcoholic and drug addict. His skin was wet with cold perspiration, pallid and waxy. Eyes wide, nasty Hawaiian-style shirt open at the neck. His hair wet and matted into thick strands at the forehead. Face unshaven, the two-day growth telling tales about the number of chins it is supposed to conceal. The girl attempts to cover her face in Pavlovian response to the flash, then gives up. Rob makes no effort to hide. He looks as if he knows the game is up, anyway. It was to be his last bender before consenting to check into rehab.

Four days earlier, Rob had been on the brink of suicide. He had been to Ireland to visit Anna Friel, his girlfriend of two weeks, who was filming with Richard E Grant and Miranda Richardson in Bray, County Wicklow. He was back in the UK for a Sunday charity soccer match, but was not exactly match-fit. When he arrived at the game he was so ill he vomited in the toilets and looked like death. Alerted to the star's pitiful state, the showbiz desks of at least two daily papers put in calls to Rob's record company. The word came back from EMI that he had a tummy bug. Unconvinced, Matthew Wright, who was then the *Daily Mirror's* showbiz columnist, got Tim Clark on the phone. Tim was in confessional mood. Yes, Rob was in big trouble. He had, indeed, been close to taking his own life at the weekend. His drinking and drugs-taking was out of control. After leaving the club, he had gone back to his new Notting Hill home with the girl. Managers Clark and Enthoven had no idea where he was. Worried for him, they contacted Jan in Stoke and brought her down to London so she could talk to him. Jan, in spite of her training as an alcohol abuse councillor could do little to help. Rob would later say, 'Mums do mum things. Councillors are very good at sorting out other people's problems. They can't sort out their own.'

What Clark didn't tell Wright was that he believed Rob had already made an attempt to kill himself. He had downed prescription drugs, mixed with coke and booze and gone into a coma. He was found at home by a friend, who slapped him around the face and coaxed him back to life. The manager did, however, break the news to Wright that Rob would be checking into a clinic to get treatment for his addictions. Clark would later claim he had been talking 'off the record' and had confided in Wright by way of asking for privacy for his client. He also claimed the *Mirror's* rival, *The Sun*, had been briefed as well, but had agreed not to print the story. Whatever the truth, Wright had a scoop, but the row would be a source of bad blood between Williams and Wright for some considerable time to come.

Rob entered Clouds House in Wiltshire in June 1997 for six weeks of drying out. He was allowed out only once to do a video shoot. For his £4,000, Rob was cut off from the rest of the world, no television, magazines, radio or books. The regime is strict, shared dormitories and even pop stars are expected to wash up after dinner. Rob was immediately placed on a 12-step programme following the Minnesota Method used by Alcoholics Anonymous. Like his fellow patients, most receiving their treatment on the NHS, Rob's first step was to be asked to admit publicly in front of the others that he was an addict. Step two is accepting and believing that a higher power can 'restore you to sanity'. His request for a room of his own was denied. He was expected to attend group therapy sessions and leave his pop star ego at the door. 'We were all addicts and fanatics,' he said of his time there. The regime may have been harsh, but Rob thrived on it. He enjoyed the experience, if only in the short term, of being just another member of the group, 'Rob, alcoholic and drug addict'. He didn't have to play the pop star part. For a man who had few friends, other than the dope-heads he had been hanging around with since his arrival in London, he found a sense of belonging he had rarely felt. He and his fellow patients would go their separate ways at the end of the six weeks, Robbie back to his life, his companions back to theirs. They, like him, had screwed up to a lesser or greater degree, but for the days he was there, those people became his world. The actual process of not drinking or taking drugs had been easier than he expected. The physical desire for them, that chemical longing, was easier to control than he imagined. The real danger would be when he was out again, back in the environment where everyone was doing it, where he was expected to be Robbie, the New Lad crazy man, the laugh-a-minute 'Mr Saturday Night'. In the clinic, he could talk about his feelings of worthlessness, his self-loathing without being given a slap on the back and the offer of another line. The whole idea was to talk about his emotions, his fears and insecurities and Rob decided he liked it. Never one to hold back on the notion of baring one's soul, here he embraced the idea with renewed vigour.

'Clouds was fantastic,' he said on his release. 'It's the sort of place that, when I have kids, I'll send them there for finishing school.' He left the clinic and went straight to Elstree, Hertfordshire, to record an edition of *Top of the Pops* he was hosting. He was straight back to his old life, but the experience had a profound effect on him. With evangelical zeal he adopted the language of analysis, the therapy-speak buzzwords, 'catharsis' and 'empowerment'. When the 12-step programme was conceived in the 1930s, the idea was for alcoholics to find God through their addiction. Rob hadn't found God, but he had discovered a new religion, practised not in church but in the consulting rooms of expensive shrinks and amid the Formica and potted plants of the AA meeting.

However, his convalescence would be short. Days after leaving Clouds, Rob came face to face with another demon that had plagued him for years, Nigel Martin-Smith. The two met for the first time since Rob's sudden departure from Take That in the wood-panelled splendour of London's High Court. Rob, head newly shaved, looking slim and healthy in Alexander McQueen suit and bug-eye shades, arrived at court looking remarkably relaxed. After the huge expense of his failed legal battle with RCA, the latest court-room encounter threatened to leave him broke if Martin-Smith proved his case that Williams owed him a percentage of his earnings. The court was told that the singer was kicked out of the group by his four band mates after he developed a taste for 'glamorous and flamboyant company, alcohol and narcotics'. In court Rob turned and winked at his adversary. It was his way of telling his former boss he feared him no more. Martin-Smith could take all the money he had earned, but he longer had any power over him.

As the court battle rumbled on, Rob was hit by another writ, this time from Tim Abbott. In a case estimated to be worth in the region of £1 million, Abbott's Proper Management company lodged a High Court writ seeking damages and £70,500 in unpaid fees. As he waited for the ruling in the Martin-Smith case, Rob was putting a brave face on things. 'If I win or lose now, it doesn't really matter,' he said. 'It's a load of dough. It could cripple me financially.

But at the end of the day, what's really the worst thing that could happen? I could lose some money. I didn't used to have any money. I could do that again.' The ruling, though, was a massive blow to Rob and his bank balance. Mr Justice Ferris ordered the singer to pay an initial £90,000 to Martin-Smith and ordered an inquiry into exactly how much Williams had earned since leaving Take That. Legal experts said they expected the damages, plus costs, to reach close to £1 million. Rob's record company laughed off claims that the ruling could bankrupt their singer. Rob, however, was not laughing. The cost of the case, plus his lost action against RCA and his ongoing legal disputes with Abbott and Kevin Kinsella had cleared him out.

CHAPTER NINE
angels

In July 2002 a 29-year-old Dubliner sat nervously in a courtroom while his solicitor told a judge his story. There was nothing out of the ordinary about the offence. His client Ray Heffernan had been caught by the police driving without insurance five months earlier. He'd been banned from driving for 12 months and fined 750 Euros (about £500). The lawyer wanted the fine reduced. Heffernan, he said, did not have much money and earned only £200 a week. He also wanted his licence back so he could visit his four-year-old daughter 50 miles away. The case was like a hundred other sob stories Judge Patricia Ryan had, no doubt, heard that week, except for one thing. Heffernan was, said his lawyer, the man who wrote "Angels".

Considering the flak Rob was taking on the legal front, it was surprising he could get out of bed in the morning. In truth, back then, it generally took a line of coke before that particular manoeuvre could be completed, but there was hope on the horizon. Despite the difficulty producers Chambers and Power had keeping Rob sober enough to record *Life Thru A Lens*, Robbie Williams's long-awaited debut album was ready. The artwork for the CD would see our hero, shaven-headed and steely-eyed in familiar pose, getting trailed by the paparazzi and a group of showbiz hangers-on. The title track had, in fact, been inspired by those famous-for-being-famous ubiquitous party-goers Tara Palmer-Tomkinson and Meg Matthews. There was little doubt in Rob's camp and at his record company EMI that those eleven tracks would decide his future. Even in the pre-*Pop Idol* days of 1997, record companies did not hang on to acts that failed to shift units. A pop star who is falling down drunk most of the time is tolerated and wrapped in cotton wool if he is making his label money. If not, it's another good reason to dump his sorry ass.

The album's release was preceded by two singles. The first, "Lazy Days", benefited from the publicity surrounding the court case with Nigel Martin-Smith. They say you should write about what you know – Rob wrote about being drunk. But what the song possessed in undeniable authenticity, it lacked in the fundamental prerequisite for a good pop song – it just wasn't memorable. It sounded like an album track, not the song that was going to kick-start a career and launch a successful album. With Rob still doing his Liam impression at the end of lines, it still sounded as if he had not decided if he wanted to be Robbie Williams or was auditioning for Noasis, the tribute band to the Gallagher brothers. The song reached number eight when EMI were hoping for a top spot. The follow-up single, "South of the Border", was released two weeks before the album, but the movement was all in the wrong direction. The song, which started life on the platform of Stoke on Trent railway station, has got shades of Aerosmith's Steve Tyler about it and Rob gives it his best Mick Jagger swagger in the opening verse. It reached number 14. It isn't difficult to imagine the sound of laughter echoing around the cavernous Cheshire country house of one Mr G Barlow.

Barlow's treatment in the bitter rant "Ego a Go Go" is reminiscent of John Lennon's post-Beatles mauling of Paul McCartney in "How Do You Sleep?". The track, brimming with hate and resentment, is a get-even assault by Rob on the man whose shadow he lived in during his boy band days. Perhaps unsurprisingly, the lyrics did not come up in the conversation the two ex-band mates had in the week the album was launched. The phone call between Rob and Barlow, the first time they had talked since Williams's departure from the group, was about a proposed Take That reunion in the wake of the death of the Diana, Princess of Wales. Despite the negotiations, Rob relished his admission that the song was 'about one of the boys'. The reunion never happened. When the Gary-Barlow-inspired Concert of Hope, which was dedicated to the late princess, took place in December 1997, Rob and Barlow performed separately. The closest they got was singing "Let It Be" with the other performers on the bill for the concert's finale. Ironically, the one-off band reunion was scuppered by Mark Owen, who was in the midst of a solo career and refused the invitation to perform with the rest of the band.

Those who doubted Rob, even those very close him, never admit it now. There was never any suspicion he wouldn't make it, they'll tell you. There were no wobbles.

'We always knew Rob had what it takes,' they say. This is, of course, rubbish. There were moments when the future of Robbie Williams as a solo entertainer was very much in the balance. By November 1997, two months after its release, *Life Thru a Lens* had sold just 30,000 copies. The singles had failed to lift sales and the album had peaked in the lower levels of the Top 20. By December it had all but disappeared, sales were minimal and it had sunk to number 104 in the charts. EMI panicked. The star for whom they had shelled out millions on wasn't selling records. The knives were out for him. Matthew Wright, whose feud with Williams had only intensified since his run-in with Tim Clark, told his *Daily Mirror* readers: 'I bet Chrysalis bosses are beginning to wonder what they paid £2 million for.' The executives from EMI, who had seen Rob wrecked at too many music business parties, were having more than doubts. Suddenly Robbie Williams was bad news and few wanted to be associated with a failed act. By the end of the year the word was already out that with minimal sales of *Life Thru a Lens* and no sign of a turnaround, Williams was on the verge of being dumped by the label. The argument, of course, goes that nobody was worried because they all knew that Rob had "Angels" in the can and the song was such a dynamite proposition that it would turn the ship around. The problem was that the song had received mixed reviews from the critics. The record company planned to pump more cash into a television advertising campaign to try to rescue something from the situation, but were talked out of it by Clark and Enthoven.

It could have been something to do with the mood of the nation after Diana's death. Maybe the record-buying public was ready for a song about salvation, redemption and celestial protection. Maybe it was just that it was right for Christmas. Maybe it was just a good record. For many switching on their radios in early December 1997, "Angels" was the first time Robbie Williams had actually registered to them. Sure, they knew he was that kid from Take That, but this was the first time he had found an audience beyond the screaming banshee that was the 'Thatter'. Coming after Elton John's reworking of "Candle in the Wind", the song seemed to carry on the theme. Important, too, was the way he sang it. This was no sound-a-like performance like "Old Before I Die". What you heard was Williams's voice and the revelation for many was that the cheeky one from Take That, the one who wasn't Gary Barlow, the pretty one or the other two, could actually sing. It became a national sport, those who had heard the song daring those who hadn't to guess the singer when it came on: 'Not that smirking one. Are you sure?' Within a year the song would have been played 42,000 times on UK radio. People wanted it played at their weddings, christenings and funerals. On the back of its enormous success, the album, languishing in the nether regions of the charts, began picking up sales. The 30,000 loyal Take That fans, who would have bought Robbie's a capella rendition of Wagner's *Ring*, were joined by an audience who would never have been seen dead buying a Take That record. It still wasn't exactly cool to buy a Robbie Williams CD, but those leaving WH Smith with the album no longer felt obliged to hide it under the copy of *Hustler*. The album finally reached number one after 28 weeks in the album charts.

Guy Chambers knows the exact date he wrote "Angels". It was the day after meeting Rob in January 1997. He had played the simple chord progression on the piano as Rob sang the lyric he had written about his Aunty Jo and Grandad Williams. The song would help to establish the pair as one of the most successful writing partnerships of their generation. In Chamber's official version of how the song came about, there is no mention of another co-writer. But this was not the beginning of the chequered history of the tune. In fact, it had started life in a Dublin attic. It came about as a result of the death of an unborn baby, later named Matthew, who had been the son of Ray Heffernan and his girlfriend Joanne Louchart. Heffernan had been living in Paris and the loss of his child in 1996 destroyed the relationship with the baby's French mother. Still grieving for his dead son and the end of his affair, he returned to his native Dublin to try to get his life back on track. In 1996, during the Christmas period, he was having a Saturday afternoon drink in the city's Globe bar when he met Robbie Williams. The singer was in the city for a holiday with his mum Jan and sister Sally. Rob, in the middle of his addictions, was in bad shape. Devastated and angry over the manner of his departure from Take That, he struck up a friendship with the Irishman who was experiencing his own turmoil. Heffernan, a keen songwriter and musician, was well known among the unsigned band brigade and pop wannabes in the Irish capital and the two men talked bands and music they liked. They got drunk together and ended up back at Heffernan's mother's house at 6 a.m. Heffernan played his new friend some songs and they decided to try their hand at writing a few tunes together.

Nothing really worked until Heffernan played Rob a song he had written upstairs at his mother's house. It was called "Angels Instead". Excited by the new tune, Rob and Heffernan worked on lyrics together.

Today, Heffernan says of his meeting with Rob: 'I was in the pub with a friend of mine. We both had bleached blond hair and white T-shirts on. Robbie came in alone and walked up to us. He asked us if we were in a boy band. We got on immediately. He is a very open guy and it was obvious he was having a lot of problems in his life. He said he was looking for a writing partner.' The course of pop history would have been changed if the pair had given up after their first attempt at penning a song together. Their first effort was unpromisingly called "The Bagpuss Complex" and was about the stuffed cat from the children's television programme. 'It wasn't a great song,' says Ray. Then the Irishman played "Angels Instead" on an acoustic guitar. 'The verse and the verse melody was mine,' says Ray. The words at the start of the chorus were mine, but the big chorus melody, the big epic bit that starts 'And through it all' came later, that was down to Rob and Guy Chambers. We recorded the song that night on a Dictaphone and it sounds really funny to listen to it now because it is basically two drunken blokes trying to sing "Angels". I think we both felt the spirituality in the song because Rob wasn't happy at the time and neither was I.'

Rob rang up Boyzone manager Louis Walsh in Dublin and asked him to set up a studio in the Irish capital so he and Heffernan could record the new song. But even after they put the song on tape in the city's STS studio, Ray was still unconvinced about its potential. 'We spent the whole day on it, but to be honest,' he says, 'I didn't particularly like the song. I always thought it was unfinished because all we had was the verse. I thought it would disappear. We actually had a dance loop on the track and it wasn't until I heard "Angels" later when Robbie recorded it with Guy that I really realized we had really missed it. When I heard that Beatles'-style piano at the beginning I knew Guy had really nailed the song. He had got it just right and he did a great job on it. I was really impressed with it.'

But Rob was thrilled with the unfinished version. The two men talked about Ray joining Rob's band and the singer invited his new friend over to England to stay with him and write some more songs. Rob returned to London and Ray travelled back to Paris to collect his possessions. 'Robbie called me and told me to come to London and gave me a number to call when I arrived,' says Ray. But, when Heffernan got to the capital, Rob was not there. 'He'd been on a massive bender, then he'd gone up to his mother's house in Stoke,' Ray adds. The Irishman stayed with a friend for a few days, but his calls and messages to Rob went un-answered, so he decided to hitchhike to Staffordshire to see his new pal. 'I didn't really know many other people in England so I just thought I'd go up and see Robbie at his mum's house,' says Ray. The problem for Heffernan was he didn't actually know where Jan lived. He ended up asking passers-by in Stoke if they knew where the star's home was. Eventually, one pointed out a house with a yellow Porsche parked outside and told him it was Jan's place. At 10 p.m. that evening the dogged Heffernan knocked on Jan's door. He was not a welcome caller. Rob invited him in, gave him a cup of tea then said to him: 'Look man, you're scaring me. Why are you following me.' Heffernan says, 'This is when I realized it had all gone pear-shaped. I honestly thought he was going to be pleased to see me, but he wasn't. He was under a lot of pressure and was doing a lot of cocaine and I think he had got paranoid.' Jan gave Heffernan £40 to stay in a local bed and breakfast and he went back to Ireland the next day. It was the last time he saw Rob.

His subsequent contact would be through Rob's management company IE Music. He was told the completed Williams–Chambers version of the song was to be included on Rob's first debut album *Life Thru a Lens*. Rob's managers Tim Clark and David Enthoven made an offer to Heffernan. He would be given a once-only payment of £10,000, and would renounce any claim to royalties from sales of the song. Heffernan says he was more interested in getting a writing credit for the song to help boost his career as a songwriter. He believed part of the agreement was that his name would be used on the single and album. 'I imagined that my name would appear as a writer under the song title on the CD sleeve,' says Ray. In fact, Heffernan's name did not appear on the album. On the jacket of the single Rob had included the dedication, 'Even fallen angels laugh last, thanks to Ray Heffernan.' 'I was very disappointed,' says Ray.

Almost a year after meeting Rob, Heffernan heard the new version of "Angels" for the first time when he went out and bought *Life Thru a Lens*. What is undeniable is that Heffernan was paid off by Williams. He also signed an agreement with Rob's management company. In court to try to get his driving–fine reduced, Heffernan's lawyer Bernard McCabe told the judge that, although the song had made Williams a fortune, Heffernan had not been so fortunate.

Like Williams, Ray had been going through his own battle with drink and drugs and had signed the deal with IE when he was in rehab. He had left Ireland at the age of 19 and had gone to Paris to work as a music therapist to autistic children as a way of trying to fight his addictions. But, when he was back in Ireland during the Christmas when he met Rob, he had fallen back into old ways. Says Ray today: 'I was drinking a lot and my drug of choice was Ecstasy. Rob gave me my first line of coke. He pulled it out of his sock where he kept it. He didn't force me to take it. I put it up my nose and was happy to do it. We were just sharing our drugs, but I did get into serious problems with coke.' Heffernan witnessed the difference between the two faces of Williams, the star and the man. Says Ray: 'He refused to answer to the name Robbie outside of the stage environment and when we would go into a club he would say, "I'll just put on my Robbie jacket".'

Williams was also, says Heffernan, deeply disturbed about his relationship with Nigel Martin-Smith. When I first met him he was really, really unhappy. I spent a few nights with him just crying in my lap,' says Ray. 'He was very, very down. He talked a lot about Nigel Martin-Smith and the anger he felt towards him. Robbie openly referred to Nigel as "Satan". There was a lot of hatred. There were serious issues there. You could see it in Robbie's face. He was carrying at lot of pain.' In his relationship with his mother, Rob was very much the junior partner, says Ray. 'Jan was very much in charge of the

Robbie Williams corporation,' he says. 'Robbie spoke with a lot of anger about his father, but Jan was the Virgin Mary. She is very protective of him and the night I stayed at their holiday house I got 20 questions from her. She is a real amateur psychologist. Robbie said to me in the taxi on the way over, "When you meet my mum, say I met you a few years ago when I was in Take That." He had to get our stories straight. She certainly called the shots. When I went to her house in Stoke to see Robbie she took control of the situation. Once she came down stairs, he shut up.'

The problems that Heffernan was facing were not helped as "Angels" went on to become a massive hit. 'I had to detach myself from it, because if I didn't I think I would have gone mad,' he says. 'It is only recently that I can listen to it and say that it is a really good Robbie Williams song because I felt a lot of anger and a lot of disappointment that I never got the acclaim for it. The song has made millions, but the money side of it has never really bothered me. What is hurtful is that Robbie won't even acknowledge me. I was part of that song and I'm still angry about that. Robbie didn't steal it from me, but I just wish he had acknowledged my involvement in it. Even so, I am so happy that the song has touched so many people and that is more important than who wrote it.'

CHAPTER 10
grace

It's what every woman wants, isn't it? To have a song written for her, dedicated to her. Imagine having your beauty immortalized as Patti Boyd did by George Harrison in "Something" and Eric Clapton's "Layla". Imagine having the power to arouse that level of emotion and inspiration.

"Sexed Up", the fifth track on *Escapology*, is a bitter song, bile with a melody, full of antipathy and resentment. A musical 'Dear John' letter, it's about getting dumped Robbie Williams-style. He pulls no punches. There's none of that 'It's not you, it's me' bullshit, no softening of the blow. He gives it you straight: 'You're chucked and here's why'. He almost spews the lines 'Screw you. I didn't like your taste. Anyway, I chose you and that's all gone to waste. It's Saturday, I'll go out and find another you.' The song ends, 'I hope you blow away, away, blow away.' In the autumn of 2002, when he sang it to an audience for the first time, Rob dedicated it to his ex-fiancée Nicole Appleton.

By January 1998 the tide was turning. At the end of the month *Life Thru a Lens* had sold 210,000 copies and was about to overtake the sales of Gary Barlow's debut album, *Open Road*. While "Angels" had sold nearly half a million copies, Barlow's latest single, "So Help Me Girl", had only managed to shift 70,000. The momentum "Angels" had given to Rob's career was enormous. A month later the album had gone double platinum and "Angels" had topped 600,000 sales. Rob's performance in February at the Brits stole the show. His *Full Monty* duet with Tom Jones lit up the night. Rob in leather suit, a Mini Me to the Welsh superstar, was a reincarnation of the 1960s version of the hip-shaking sensation. His show-stealing routine provided the ultimate evidence that Williams, despite his continuing addictions, was the most natural, most assured stage performer of his generation. There was no one to touch him – nobody even came close. Jones was an instant fan. 'That boy has so much energy he makes me feel young again. In fact, he made everyone in the room feel younger,' the superstar said. 'I think he is one of the most talented performers in Britain today.' Likewise, his first appearance on *Parkinson*, while promoting "Angels", was a bravura display. Rob going round the back of the host's chair, pointing at the giggling inter-viewer, looking down the camera and exclaiming 'Look Mum, Parky'. It was TV heaven, what everyone who goes on the show wants to do, but few possess Williams's guts or style. The gesture said, 'Hey, look at me, I've made it'. Rob, with childlike enthusiasm, had won over the audience with his seemingly effortless charm. In front of fellow guest Ewan McGregor, he even bragged about the film parts he was being offered. He came over as gauche but endearing, like a kid fibbing that his dad played for Liverpool. Those who witnessed those two performances were there at the birth of a phenomenon – Robbie Williams Mark Two was born.

Rob had met Nicole Appleton, singer in girl band All Saints, six months earlier back stage in a television studio. The couple had exchanged pleasantries about each other's music and then gone their separate ways. They were both on the bill of the Concert of Hope at Battersea Power Station and during rehearsals Nicole invited Rob to a party to celebrate her 23rd birthday. He turned up early with his flatmate Charlie and over half-pints of lager, he and Nicole spent the night chatting. They posed for a picture taken on the Polaroid camera Nicole had received as a birthday present and she was already in love. The next day she got her manager to get her Rob's number, but was too scared to ring him. Before she mustered up the courage to call, the newspapers revealed that Rob had been out on a date with blonde TV presenter Denise Van Outen. *The Big Breakfast* hostess had sent a Rob a bird with a card saying, 'Can I be your bird?'. But Rob was more interested in seeing the younger of the two Appleton sisters again. Nicole got drunk and decided to phone him anyway. Pleased to hear from her, Rob told Nicole he was going to a studio in the country the next day to do some recording. He invited her down for dinner. She fought her way out of London in a taxi and through the snow to get to the Buckinghamshire studio. That evening Rob sang to her from the sound booth and the two ate together, went to the pub and got drunk. It was too late for Nicole to get back to London, so they slept together back-to-back in Rob's bed. The following morning as Nicole headed back to London, the front page of *The Sun* proclaimed Rob's love for Denise.

Rob didn't ring Nicole for a week. Their second date was unconventional. On December 29, Rob phoned her from a party he was at in north London. He was wasted and wanted her to come over to get him. She arrived to find him lying on a sofa in a terrible state. She helped him back to his place and, from that moment, the two were an item. Four days later a photographer, waiting outside Rob's house, got a picture of Nicole leaving in the morning and the story was out. Rob had previously been linked to Spice Girl Mel C. Although she would later claim they had never been a couple, he let a friend reveal that Sporty had become 'a bit obsessed' with him. As a result the other Spice Girls would cut him dead whenever their paths crossed.

A little over a month after they started dating, Rob and Nicole were both on the bill at the Brits. Rob was up for four gongs, but left empty-handed, All Saints' "Never Ever" won two awards, for best British single and video. By now, the couple were a regular sight on the party scene or treating diners to passionate displays over their food at London's Oxo Tower restaurant. Nicole, head over heels in love, gushed to *The Sun*, 'He is one of the sweetest people I have ever met and I can't imagine how he has managed to cope with all the attention. He has a reputation for being wild, but that is not the Robbie I know. He is so much fun. Robbie is always going to be in the public eye because he was in Take That and that does put pressure on a relationship. He really makes me laugh and I hope we last a long time, though we are both too young to be committed yet.' A month later, Nicole was pregnant with Rob's baby. She made the discovery while in Vancouver on a promotional tour with All Saints. She and her band mate Melanie Blatt both found out they were expecting on the same day. Nicole worked out she must have conceived on Valentine's Day.

In her book *Together*, Nicole revealed that she rang Rob in London at 2 a.m. At first he was silent when she told him she had some news for him. But her new boyfriend was instantly delighted when she revealed she was expecting his child. 'That's great, babe,' he said. 'I'm really happy about it. It's what I want.' But, claimed Nicole, as soon as news of the joint pregnancies in her band become known to her management and record company, she was put under pressure to have a termination. While Melanie stood firm and refused to give in to the coercion, Nicole found herself being forced into a corner by those around her.

When Nicole arrived back in the UK, Rob took her to see his grandmother Betty in Stoke. The baby, he told Nicole, was saving his life. They decided that if the baby was a girl they would call her Grace. Rob wrote a song for his unborn child, which would appear on his second album *I've Been Expecting You*. It included the lines, 'Grace, I'm not yet born. Come embrace a soul that's torn. I've got so much to give you.' What Nicole didn't say in her book was that, despite the hearts and flowers image she paints of the relationship and despite its relative infancy, it had already been beset by problems. Two weeks before finding out she was pregnant, the couple had had their first of many break-ups. Despite their positions as pop players at the pinnacle of UK showbusiness, their glamorous lifestyles, the cars, the clothes, they were, in private, both prone to childishness and alcohol-fuelled bickering. Those around them would squirm with embarrassment as the two, like kindergarten toddlers, would quarrel publicly about everything from which CD they each wanted to play, to which restaurant they should go to. Nicole might only have been 23 and Rob a year older but, away from the spotlight, they both appeared much younger. Both had reputations as party animals, but as a couple they appeared to be strangely naive and unworldly. They would pass hours in Rob's 'playroom' at the top of his house playing *Star Wars* games or pretending to be DJs.

The relationship had not been helped by the long periods the couple spent apart as they sought to consolidate their burgeoning careers. Rob was promoting his new single "Let Me Entertain You" and preparing for a sell-out national tour, which was due to begin in May. Meanwhile, All Saints were in the US carrying out an exhausting PR onslaught. By early March the word was already out that the pair had broken up. They were both privately confessing that their busy lives had put the relationship under terminal pressure. They were conducting their love affair by phone and decided to take a break from each other. Nicole's announcement that she was pregnant had given new life to the relationship, but it was still not without problems. Rob was still drinking heavily and often with Nicole, but unlike with Jacqui Hamilton-Smith, both Jan and Pete liked their son's girlfriend, and felt she was a positive influence on him. Jan said at the time: 'I'd love Nicole as my daughter-in-law. She would be my choice for Robert. She has a lovely attitude and a lovely family and she makes Robert happy. But I can't say who he can marry. It's up to him.'

By April, Nicole was in New York and was cracking under

the pressure to get rid of the baby that could stall her career just as it was taking off. From her rented apartment in Trump Tower, she phoned Rob in tears and told him she was going to go ahead with the abortion. Rob told her he would take the first Concorde flight out of Heathrow and join her in the morning. The next day was spent with Nicole in tears wrestling with her conscience over her decision. Rob had been supportive. He had not tried to persuade her either way. But after a sleepless night, he escorted his lover to the Manhattan offices of a private abortion clinic. The couple were told Nicole was four months pregnant. Then, while Rob sat in the waiting room outside, Nicole was led next door while his baby was removed from her body. Nicole, who was awake during the procedure, fainted. When she came round Rob was with her. Outside, a limousine was waiting to take them back to the apartment. The following day they flew back to London on Concorde. To this day, Nicole wrote in her book, she doesn't know if Rob ever forgave her for aborting his child.

While his personal life was being put through the grinder, Rob's career was bang on track. "Let Me Entertain You", as much a mission statement as a record, had got to number three in the UK charts. In June, Sky TV made Rob's sell-out gig at the Forum in London its first ever pay-per-view pop concert. Fans could pay £9.95 to watch *Robbie Williams – Live in Your Living Room*. He was in world-beating mood. 'Things are phenomenal at the moment, but it's no surprise,' he boasted. 'I wouldn't have started out in music if I didn't think I could be the biggest in the world. It's all there for me as long as I stay tip top.'

He was well aware that the biggest threat to his career did not come from a sudden lack of interest from the public. The Robbie bandwagon would not suddenly run out of steam, the fans would not get tired of the monkey-faced rascal as quickly as they had become sold on him. No, Rob was all too conscious that he was the master of his own destiny. There was never any doubt in his mind from the moment he walked out on stage as the Artful Dodger and drew that gasp from the audience, that audible sign of approval. Rob knew what he had was special. With the trained senses of one instinctively aware of the nature of his own gift, he quietly studied the others around him in the business. He saw little sign from his nearest rivals of anything resembling his ability to manipulate, to move an audience the way he could. He could, of course, lose the lot, but it would be down to him. The demons were still there, the drink and drugs. That fear remains with him to this day, the almost phobic terror of throwing it all away, which has brought the true moments of clarity even as his addictions threatened to submerge him. That dread has made him step back from the cliff edge when he has been closest to blowing it. The knowledge of what he was wasting has always been there in the background, nagging, cajoling, taunting. It has saved his life.

Given that his battle with the bottle had more than a few very public rounds to go, it was, in hindsight, a tad optimistic to be talking of his drinking in the past tense. But in the summer of 1998 Rob was confident he had beaten the urge to get drunk. 'Staying away from drink was a day-to-day struggle for a long time,' he said in June that year. 'I think about it all the time, every day, without fail. In the last couple of weeks my life has become a joy again and I now think about my music instead of drink. If I want a beer I have one. I just don't feel like one often. I know I fucked up big time. But the great thing about the British public is they know that and they'll forgive you if you're good.'

The bond with the public has always been at the core of the Robbie Williams phenomenon. Despite the fame, the mansions, the millions in the bank, he has always seemed to pull off the illusion that he is one of us, of the people and for the people. There are those who are sceptical. Here, after all, is a man rich beyond the wildest imaginings of his fans, a star since he left school, a man who has been pandered to, pampered and mollycoddled. If Rob from Stoke ever existed he was left behind with the dole-queue losers, the teenage parents, the pay-pack peasants, as the newly incarnated Robbie headed for Manchester and fame. He might look like one of us, he might sound like one of us, but Robbie, they say, is an impostor; a walking, talking replicant from Planet Celebrity, pulling a fast one on a gullible public.

Certainly Rob was beginning worryingly to show signs of a conversion from civilian to luvvie. He was starting to exhibit the side effects of one too many lie-downs on the couches of celebrity therapists. With earnest dedication he had become schooled in therapy-speak. His conversations were peppered with the telltale words and phrases. He had 'empowered himself', he began telling interviewers. He had done some 'serious work' on himself and, apparently straight-faced, had uttered the immortal line: 'I just decided to take a swim in Lake Me.' He also took a fair amount of flak in the Press for describing himself as 'an artist' and after one successful album stating categorically, 'I can actually write songs that stand alongside some of the great song-writers of my generation.'

His skill was, and remains, his ability to turn it all into a joke, even at his own expense. His tour was appropriately entitled 'The Ego has Landed'. Rob was wowing the fans and, for the first time, winning over the hitherto dubious highbrow critics who couldn't believe that the former member of *Take That* could make decent records. *Life Thru a Lens* was nominated for a Mercury Music Prize.

Despite its stormy nature, the relationship with Nicole had survived the trauma of her abortion. It also stood firm in the face of allegations from lap dancer Sandy Palermo that she had given a private show for Rob at his Notting Hill home. In the early summer the couple became engaged. Rob proposed to Nicole when she arrived back at his home at 5 a.m. after a flight in from Japan. Bleary-eyed, he got out of bed and down on one knee to present her with an antique emerald-cut diamond ring. They both cried with joy. The couple went on holiday to St Tropez to celebrate their impending marriage. They would soon be separated again, however, as All Saints began a tour of Argentina, Mexico and Brazil. The couple resumed their long-distance relationship with daily phone calls, but Rob was growing increasingly tired of the separations. Seven weeks after he asked Nicole to be his wife, he called off their love affair in a short and brutal phone call. Nicole had landed in Rio to find a voice-mail message from Rob waiting for her at her hotel. In her book she told how the relationship had seemed fine six days earlier when she left Rob in London. But in the intervening week his attitude had changed. When Nicole rang her fiancé back the conversation was short. Rob told her they didn't see each other enough. He was confused, but he had made up his mind. It was over. Nicole put down the phone and began to howl.

The Sun broke the story that the relationship was over, but reported that it had been Nicole who had called it off. Rob told the paper he had been left in tears over the split. 'I'm totally gutted,' he said. 'Nicole means the world to me but it has been so difficult with her being away on tour so much. I still hope we can sort things out. We're very good friends and we speak on the phone all the time. But for the moment it's all off.' The break lasted until Nicole returned home to the UK. While she was crying for her lost love, Rob looked like he was having more success in getting over their split. He took off again to the South of France and was photographed with a gaggle of beach beauties. He was also said to have gone on a mammoth booze trip to Puerto Banus in Spain where he picked up two girls during 24-hour drinking sessions. Once back in the UK, Danish barmaid Linnea Dietrichson claimed Rob took her back to his pad for sex after meeting her at London's DTPM club. Nicole, meanwhile, was being drenched at Blackpool doing a Radio One Roadshow. Rob famously described himself as 'the loneliest man in the world' and got his flatmate Charlie to ring Nicole to tell her that he still loved her despite their break-up. Then Rob rang himself to invite her out to dinner at showbiz eatery Nobu. The couple got drunk and Nicole was photographed taking a ride on Rob's back as they emerged from a bar. A few days later Rob proposed again.

This time the circumstances were less romantic. They were in the back of a taxi on the way to a party in London's less than glitzy East End.

In the meantime, Rob had a career to pursue. The second album, *I've Been Expecting You,* was in the can and ready for release in the autumn. The relationship had inspired several of the songs on the record. "Win Some Lose Some" features Nicole's voice purring: 'I love you baby'. She had recorded the love message on a keyring with built-in sampler she gave to Rob as a present. "Heaven From Here" and "Grace" were also written about his romance with the singer. But while Rob was busy eulogizing about how Nicole had become his muse, the lyrics told a different story. While Nicole's disembodied voice ran on a loop at the start of "Win Some Lose Some", the words spoke of a relationship already doomed. The first line goes 'We didn't think it'd last beyond summer' and the final chorus repeats the lines, 'Now it's gone, you win some, you lose some'.

By the end of 1998, Rob and Nicole were watching what was left of their relationship die a slow, painful death. His attachment to the bottle was, however, as strong as ever. He was likely to go on marathon binges, especially if he felt he had good cause – a bad day, a row with Nicole or his mum. Few close to the two singers could keep up with whether they were on or off. In December Rob had been doing a show in Amsterdam and Nicole flew out to be with him. He sent a thousand red roses to her hotel room, but the gesture was not enough to convince either of them that they had any real future together. On Christmas Day he was out of it and angry after a day drinking in the pub near her parent's home. They had a fierce row and he walked out, saying he wasn't coming back. He checked into a faceless London hotel desperate and alone. In the bar of the Stakis Hotel, Edgware, a slurring Rob proceeded to tell a bunch of strangers the full gory details of his latest bust-up with Nicole. He invited four guys to his room and then he disappeared. He passed out on a sofa in a corridor and was photographed, plastered and pathetic, by fellow guests who were kind enough to smear him with toothpaste and shaving foam before flogging the snaps to *The Sun*.

I've Been Expecting You went to the top of the album chart. The second single taken from it, "Millennium", a cynically successful bid by Williams and Chambers to cash in on the excitement of the upcoming year 2000, became his first UK number one. The album had at its heart the theme of lost relationships. "No Regrets", which featured Rob's heroes The Pet Shop Boys, sounds like a musical goodbye to an ex-lover. In reality, it was Rob's farewell to his four Take That comrades. It even re-visits the band's fall-out with Jan over her insistence on keeping tabs on Rob's money, with the line, 'Felt things were going wrong when you didn't like my mother.' "Karma Killer" a scathing, vitriolic tirade, was described as Rob's revenge on those who had doubted his talent. In fact it is a hate-filled attack on Take That manager Nigel Martin-Smith. 'Why haven't you managed to die yet? You could prop up the bar in hell', Rob taunts. 'I hope you choke on your Bacardi and Coke'. The theme is a common one – Rob unable to forgive, unwilling to be magnanimous in victory. Old scores are there to be settled, then the wounds re-opened and settled again. Williams, doesn't do forgiveness. He is obsessively drawn to revisit the failure of his personal relationships, to pick over the carcasses and make soup out of them.

CHAPTER ELEVEN
world domination

On a scrub patch of burnt land a young man in light-coloured T-shirt, baggy shorts, trainers and baseball cap was playing keep-up with a leather football. Chest out, elbows bent, palms facing up behind him, his eyes were fixed on the ball 18 inches in front of his body. The gaggle of kids surrounding him had their eyes on the stranger. They didn't have a clue who he was, but the ball he brought with him had broken down the barriers of language and race. For the moment, at least, he was one of them.

A day earlier, Rob had frozen when, not long off his plane from London, he was confronted by a phalanx of soldiers, guns ready, twitchy. His All Saints girlfriend Nicole Appleton had wept when Rob headed for the airport for the flight to Sri Lanka. The country was at war. She thought he'd be killed. Rob was not completely convinced he would get home in one piece either. A few days before he began the trip, which was due to end in the northern district of Jaffna, a province claimed as their own by the notorious Tamil Tigers, a bomb had killed a group of people that included the mayor. Rob was given the chance to bail out, to give the trip a miss, but decided to go anyway. The decision to join a UNICEF mission to Sri Lanka to help with a polio vaccination programme had been made at the last minute. Rob asked his friend and fellow musician Ian Dury if he could tag along when the singer, himself a polio victim, had told Rob about his work for the charity and how it took him on regular trips to the war-torn region. In the autumn of 1998 Rob was number one with "Millennium" and was just the right man to help publicize the work of the charity.

At the eleventh hour the trip to Jaffna was cancelled as the United Nations said it would be unsafe because of the recent bombing. Rob, Ian and the UNICEF team made their way to impoverished Vavuniya instead. Rob was administering doses of the inoculation to babies using a pipette when a man arrived clutching a Take That album for him to autograph. He was one of only a handful who were aware of the superstar status of the ordinary-looking guy in the UNICEF cap who, a few minutes earlier, had been playing football with the children. But the tentacles of celebrity stretch even to these far-flung outposts, beyond the gun-toting soldiers to the makeshift homes and rows of skinny kids. Rob was in the country primarily to use his celebrity to raise awareness of the campaign, pose for a few pictures with the babies, and use his fame to pass the message back home. But there was another reason Rob wanted to make the trip. It was a chance, he believed, to make some sense of his own existence, to work out who he was when he wasn't being Robbie Williams, pop star. There, among the smiling kids, who wanted nothing more from him than a kick-about on a dusty strip of land, Rob was hoping to bring back memories of a life before fame, before the money, the fans, the business changed him, defined him. 'I'm not in Sri Lanka to get rich,' he said. 'I'm here because I want to put my life into place. What I worry about at home doesn't matter. I want to see people smile in the face of adversity. Does that sound awfully shallow? I don't want to sound selfish but I do want to remember what life was like before I was famous.'

A few days earlier, as he prepared to fly out of the UK, Rob was spelling out his feelings about the impending trip. 'I don't think I'm going to come back from this trip,' he said. 'Don't get me wrong. I just think, either I'll get shot or I'll come back a changed man. Yeah, changed, that's what I need right now. It's like I've reached number one and I'm thinking what have people said about me?' His candour was admirable. Yes, he wanted to help those kids in that dangerous place, but this journey was about more than that. But was his life so soulless? Was there such a lack of meaning in his existence that he was prepared to risk taking a bullet to find the answers he so desperately sought? Frighteningly, that did, indeed, appear to be the case. The trip was, of course, well marshalled, the risks minimized, security was in place, but significantly, in Rob's mind at least, the threat was real and that was the important thing. He needed to feel he was putting himself in danger, as if that way he would have some heightened sense of himself, as if that way he could put his life back home in some sort of context. Here he was at number one in the charts, his dreams had come true, and those who doubted him when he was a washed-up, drugged-up boy-band reject had been silenced. The point had been proved to Nigel Martin-Smith, Gary

Barlow and the others, but even after all this, even as he achieved the fame and respect he had hankered after his whole life, he was still unhappy, still unfulfilled, still striving for something he had not yet identified. His proposed solution seemed simplistic. Did he really expect that here, amid the poverty, the shantytowns and the sun-dried squalor that he was going to find his happiness in the human misery of others? Would it make everything OK? Would he appreciate his wealth and his fame, count his blessings and thank his lucky stars? Is that the cure for depression? Must you experience the suffering of children in Sri Lanka or push yourself to the outer reaches of sanity with the help of the bottle or a bag of drugs before you know that what you've got is worth having in the first place?

Rob seemed hopeful that he could be changed by the journey. 'I want to be enriched. There's a side to the industry I'm in which can make me feel bitter. A pessimist sits on my shoulder who says: "What you do doesn't mean anything." Because of what happened to me in Take That, success brings a pain with it. I relate success to sadness.' As Rob and the UNICEF team were about to leave, a man came up to him with a small child. He wanted Rob, a stranger, to take the little boy, his three-year-old grandson, with him back to England for a happier life.

Two months later, as Rob lay comatose on the corporate soft furnishings of the Stakis Hotel in London, it appeared little had been resolved in his mind. His relationship with Nicole was over bar the shouting and the poison-pen lyrics. If his analysis that success would only bring pain was true, he was in for a miserable time. At the beginning of the New Year it was announced that he had been nominated for a record-breaking six Brit Awards. The nominations were a reward for the combined sales of 2.3 million for *Life Thru A Lens* and *I've Been Expecting You*, making him Britain's highest-selling act of 1998. Included in the list of categories in which Rob was named were: Best British Album for *I've Been Expecting You*, Best British Male Solo Star, Best Single for "Angels" and Best British Video for the James Bond-inspired "Millennium". The transformation from 'Loser of the Year' at the 1995 *Smash Hits* awards to main man was complete. Rob was hailed as a star reborn with a phoenix-like resurrection from the ashes of his Take That career. He was the fat addict, who had cleaned himself up, got into shape, taken on the world and won. But the story was a little too tidy, a bit too easy. In truth Rob, although he looked good again, was still far from calling time on his career as a celebrity pisshead. One journalist who interviewed him at the time was so concerned about his behaviour he phoned Williams's record company to tell them he had seen at first hand Jimi Hendrix and Brian Jones throw their lives away. 'If you don't sort this out, he'll be with them by the end of the year,' he warned.

What was true was that everybody wanted a piece of Rob. Everyone wanted to be touched by, or at least catch a glimpse of, his celebrity gold dust. His tour of 24 major arenas in 13 cities at the start of 1999 sold out in less than four hours. When he appeared on the bill of Prince Charles's birthday show at the Lyceum Theatre in London, the Prince asked him what other engagements he had been forced to cancel to attend the huge charity show. 'Nothing, apart from world domination,' was Rob's cocky reply. At February's

Brits Rob won three of the awards he had been nominated for: Best Male Solo Artist, Best Single and Best British Video. He dedicated his win to his mum. 'I feel really, really happy and I know my mum will be really proud of me which is great because I would not be anywhere without her,' he said. 'I've made a lot of mistakes, so many I can't remember half of them. My mum always believed in me and thankfully so did a few others and I sorted myself and got back to doing what I want to do, which is to entertain people.' Rob performed "Millennium" with 150 dancers and leapt 50 feet from the roof of the London's Docklands Arena in a stunt that had the audience screaming. He had to have acupuncture during rehearsals to calm his nerves and by the end of the evening he was so wrecked on free vodka that his final acceptance speech consisted of holding up a hastily scrawled note with the words: 'Legless. Thank You'. After the show he went home with Jan for a post-party dinner of beans on toast. He had been so drunk that when he awoke the following morning he could not remember how many awards he had won. Jan knew the battle was not over, but for the moment she was content with the progress her son had made in his struggle to overcome his addictions. 'I'm really glad the bad days are behind us,' she said. 'They were very bad. Whenever your children are hurting and suffering it is as sad for the parent as it is for the child, no matter what age. What we found with Robert was that he was ill and it is an illness when you have a problem with alcohol or drugs. When you have that illness it's hard enough to deal with it in private. As a mum I found it really, really hard when I opened a paper in the morning or somebody would post something through my door with a photograph of him from a paper. But I will say in fairness to Robert, he shared such a lot with me that it helped me very clearly to understand what was happening to him.' During the depth of his addiction to cocaine, Rob had begged his mother to try the drug so she could know the nature of its control over him. Jan, who was used to counselling addicts in her job, refused. 'Whatever we do in our lives we take responsibility for it,' she said. 'He has done so well to address the problems he has had. He is a very strong young man.'

No more than ten days after his Brits triumph Rob still appeared to be having trouble with his reformed image. The battle he was so obviously still fighting was thrown into sharp focus during two consecutive nights at Wembley Arena. During the Saturday night show Rob had been on top of his game. He gave a blistering performance, wowing the fans with his singing and his sharp humour. The previous night had been a different story. Rob, looking the worse for wear, passed the evening smoking, swearing and showing his backside to the audience. Those who witnessed his incoherent ramblings were left in little doubt that the star had clearly spent some time prior to the show in his own hospitality area. He was also still trying to come to terms with his split from Nicole Appleton. During a Newcastle gig he used the audience as his confessor, telling how he had jetted back from his lads' holiday the previous summer in the hope of rekindling his relationship with her. 'I rang Nic and this is what I said,' he confided to his fans. He then launched a knockabout version of the Take That hit "Back For Good". But at the end of the song he shouted: 'And she still told me to get lost!' At the same time he was admitting that there was no hope of rekindling the love affair. 'When you're 25, commitment is a miracle. I am as fickle as anyone my age. People want security from me and I am not in the right mind to give it at the moment especially in the world I live in. I've got the devil in me. I don't know if it's abnormal or it's just what 25-year-olds feel, but I can't trust myself,' he said.

Ironically, given the scale of his success, there were already those who were predicting the fall from grace of the nation's top act. Rob's collaboration with the Pet Shop Boys sounded like them, not him, claimed *The Observer's* Emma Forrest. 'The John Barry pastiches are flat. The attempts at heavy rock are stodgy. Every single covers a new genre, but more and more half-heartedly.' It was true that much of the material was derivative, but Guy Chambers is unapologetic about it. He is happy to list the artists who inspired *I've Been Expecting You*. "Stalkers Day Off" is, he says, influenced by Brian Wilson of the Beach Boys. "Millennium" is based around John Barry's theme to the James Bond film *You Only Live Twice* with an added hip hop beat. On "Win Some Lose Some", the songwriters had, says Chambers, gone for a Blondie or Squeeze-style 1980s sound. "Karma Killer" was inspired, he says, by Queen's massive hit "Killer Queen". "Stand Your Ground" was an attempt to ape the sound of the Beatles's *White Album* and Jimi Hendrix.

But this musical painting by numbers didn't stop there. In "Man Machine", Rob sings, 'I'm a man machine, drinking gasoline'. Compare that to a line from Guns'N Roses song "Night Train" from their 1987 release *Appetite for Destruction*. On that track Axel Rose sings: 'I'm a mean machine, been drinking gasoline'. The song "Jesus in a Camper Van" was to land Rob with a legal dispute over royalties. He was accused of using lyrics from the song "I am the Way (New York Town)" by American singer Loudon Wainwright III. The singer threatened to force Williams's record company EMI to take copies of *I've Been Expecting You* off the shelves if the royalties row was not resolved.

At the beginning of 1999 Rob and his managers Tim Clark and David Enthoven were looking beyond the domination of the UK charts and increasing success in Europe. Rob seemed to have everything in his armoury needed to launch an assault on the US. His music, essentially middle-of-the road, should, they concluded, appeal to US radio stations and would the Yanks be any more immune to the mischievous charm of the loveable Englishman than anyone else? It seemed not. "Angels" had already gained a lot of airplay in the States and *I've Been Expecting You* had become the biggest-selling import at Tower Records in Los Angeles. Barely two weeks into the New Year Rob was in Los Angeles showcasing his talents to an invited audience of music business big shots at Hollywood's Lucky Seven club close to Capitol Records famous headquarters. Rob was keen to distance himself from his former friends Oasis whose hell-raising had not been well received in the US. 'I'm nothing like my in-bred cousins from Manchester who like to spit on the audience,' he told the assembled guests. The dig was another salvo in the entertaining war of words between the Gallagher brothers and Rob. Liam had taken to describing his new best enemy as 'Tubby-arsed Williams'. Rob told the crowd of music executives and producers, 'I've always identified more with classy singers such as Frank Sinatra and Dean Martin and tonight you have made me feel a little closer to them.'

Rob's return to the UK coincided with the failure of his attempt in the Court of Appeal to have Nigel Martin-Smith's High Court victory overturned. The court ruled Rob would have to pay the £90,000 royalties Martin-Smith said he was owed, plus the close to £1 million costs of the case. Such was Rob's hatred of the man who had discovered him that he was prepared to fight on for four months after the case had been lost. The royalties Martin-Smith wanted were a trifling amount compared to the legal costs Rob ran up in his determination that his enemy would not get the upper hand. Worse, the judges, unconvinced by Williams's argument, had also given the manager the right to sue the singer for the money he could have earned if he had been allowed to act as his manager during the six months' notice period Rob was obliged to give his former boss. Martin-Smith commented that he had 'pity' for his one-time protégé. 'On a personal level I am pleased that Robbie had continued success after Take That,' he said. 'But I feel those who have only heard Robbie's account of events would be very disillusioned if they knew the whole story. I've great pity for Robbie. I was very fond of him, but he's not the same lad I took off the dole and made into a star.'

Rob had been so down after the case that he phoned Danish barmaid Linnea Dietrichson with whom he was supposed to have had a scene at his west London home. She claimed he told her his relationship with Nicole was over as he attempted to persuade her to resume their, hitherto, purely physical affair. Rob, she said, had phoned her at 2 a.m. sounding very low and told her: 'I need you to nurse me through the night. I really do.'

CHAPTER TWELVE
the ego has landed

If the embittered lyrics of *Escapology*'s "Sexed Up" would not find public expression for another three years, the sentiment that gave life to them, fed and nurtured them, can be traced back to the spring of 1999. Word of his skirt-chasing and reports that Rob had been desperately trying to woo Irish singer Andrea Corr went down badly with Nicole. Rob had sent £250-worth of red roses and one white stem to the *Top of the Pops* studio where Andrea was performing with a note borrowing the words from her band's worldwide hit "What Can I Do To Make You Love Me". With the wounds of their failed relationship still raw, Nicole's revenge was swift and brutal. The secret of the baby and the abortion would remain between them for some time to come until Nicole wrote her autobiography in 2002. So the real venom of her attack on her former lover would only be fully understood and felt by the two people who terminated their unborn child at that Manhattan clinic. Suddenly Nicole's mood altered. The good wishes the couple sent each other through the pages of the newspapers were no more.

Her change of heart was the result of a series of ultimately tawdry reunions between the pair. The first time, having met in London's trendy Met Bar, Nicole had taken up Rob's offer to go back to his home. After treating passers-by to the sight of them kissing energetically in his living room, they retreated to his bedroom. A month later the scene was repeated after dinner at star hangout Titanic. But despite the passion of their reunion sex, Rob's post-coital demeanour had been less that attentive. He had seemed keen to get rid of her afterwards. Her calls went ignored and weren't returned. Feeling used and sullied, Nicole's bitterness towards her former lover began to smoulder and flame. Her resentment exploded with words calculated to wound and hurt the man who had once called her his 'saviour'.

'It's over. I would never have children with him and I hope he reads that,' an angry Nicole declared, 'He is too crazy and too unstable. The father of my children will have to have a normal mind and a normal life. His life just isn't real. He actually leads a pathetic life.' When the time came to write her book Nicole firmly blamed her decision to terminate her pregnancy on the commercial pressure applied by her management and record company. Twelve months after the actual event, however, she appeared to be telling a very different story. The subtext, truly understood only by those privy to the secret the couple had kept from the world, was that Nicole had taken the decision to abort the child she was carrying because she did not want Rob as the father of her children. What else was he think on reading those words? Had the talk about the coercion, applied by the corporate bean counters, desperate not to risk their money-spinning discovery, been a smokescreen? Was the real reason she had walked into that sterile, faceless building to have their child aborted that she feared the prospect of the messed-up Rob as the father to the child he had already named and sung to? There was worse to come as Rob read on. Nicole spoke about baby Lilyella, the child that her All Saints co-star Melanie Blatt discovered she was having the same day as Nicole found out she was pregnant. Nicole said, 'I just think when I see Lily that you think you've got it all, but there is so much more to look forward to. I want to see what my baby looks like, but I'm not jealous of Mel. I'm definitely not ready yet. I did want a child before the year 2000. But then I thought maybe it would be better if it was born in 2000.'

Rob, too, must have wondered what his baby would look like. He would never know. Nicole's words, even on the face of it, resentful and sour, were, with the knowledge they shared, doubly cruel. Revenge, Rob has learnt, is a dish best served cold.

The campaign to break America was gaining momentum, but the best-laid plans of Clark and Enthoven were being put in jeopardy by Rob's behaviour. A tour of Europe was called off with the record company blaming a viral infection for Rob's failure to show up for the dates. The reality was that actually getting him on stage was often a major battle for his harassed handlers. Their claims that Rob was just unwell were a desperate attempt to deflect attention from the real problem. With the US beckoning, they could not afford to admit that the singer, who a couple of months earlier had boasted to US industry bigwigs that he was the clean-living face of Britpop, seemed to be putting away more booze and drugs than the Gallagher brothers put together. With the cancellation of the European gigs at the last minute, the rumours that Rob had gone seriously off the rails began to get louder. The gossip culminated with one newspaper asking. 'Where's Robbie'. Rob replied to the increasing speculation about his state with a call to Radio One DJ Jamie Theakston. He told Theakston he had not gone missing, but was recovering from cuts and bruises he sustained after falling off a quad bike. There was no truth in the rumours he had returned to his old ways, he told the DJ. In fact he had not had a drink for a month.

The reality was, however, startlingly different. The European tour had been scrapped after Rob steadfastly refused to go on stage for the opening gig in Stockholm. As the crowd waited expectantly for their hero to emerge, Rob was involved in a stand-off with his team. In a state of near panic, they were desperately trying to persuade the star of the show that he should not let down his fans – and cost himself close to half a million pounds in the process. For an hour, while a hotline to the London offices of his management company was kept open, Guy Chambers, his band, the tour manager and his PA Gabby Chelmicka, pleaded with Rob to go out in front of his fans. He would relent and say he would do the gig then change his mind again. In the end, with the Swedish crowd clamouring for the show to begin, they were forced to go out on stage and tell them the concert was off.

Rob's state of mind in Stockholm was the legacy of, even by his own standards, some legendary high-living three nights previously. On the final leg of a promotional tour of the US, Rob had done a show in Austin, Texas. After the gig he hit the town and the bottle. He ended up at his hotel with a small group of willing girls and continued the party with the help of vodka and an endless supply of A-grade cocaine. The following morning Rob, still stoned and fighting a losing battle with gravity, was carried through the airport for a flight direct to Sweden for the start of his European tour. He had begged David Enthoven and Tim Clark to take him with them back to London. But his managers persuaded the star to make the trip to Stockholm and Rob crashed out in his first-class seat all the way across the Atlantic. Once in Stockholm, the crew had a day and half to get the singer in a fit state to go on stage. However, so massive had his Texan binge been that, as the clock ran down to the start of the show, Rob, suffering the effects of hangover and withdrawal, did not feel like entertaining anyone. He also complained his throat was hurting. The final straw came with a piece of prima donna theatre only the biggest stars feel able to perform. At the venue before the gig, Rob discovered two of his favourite crew members were not due to be working on the tour. With that discovery he called off the gig, told the tour manager he wasn't going on and went back to the hotel. Later that night he had more bad news for his team. It was not just Sweden he wouldn't be playing: he was cancelling the whole European tour.

Rob flew home to his mum while EMI peddled the line that he was still fighting the mysterious viral infection. But somebody appeared to have forgotten to tell Rob about the smokescreen. A few days later he was photographed playing football with a Stoke amateur side. 'He's certainly ill. That's not in dispute,' said a rattled EMI spokesman. Rob might have been ill, but it wasn't with the seemingly stubborn bug. His management and label were fighting an increasingly uphill struggle to keep a lid on his constant drinking and drug taking while trying to fend off a suspicious Press. Even his old friend Elton John was having concerns about Rob's health. 'I don't know exactly what's going on, but I'm hearing things about him,' said the Rocket Man. 'I just hope he sorts himself and looks after himself. I'm really concerned.' The assault on the States was being cranked up another notch. In private, Clark and Enthoven were hoping that the self-preservation mechanism Rob had previously displayed when perilously close to the precipice would kick in when they needed it most. He would step back from the edge, get his head together and give them a fighting chance. They also knew that any British star, wanting really to break through in America, would have to invest an enormous amount of hard work and commitment in the venture. On the face of it Rob did not look in the sort of shape to pull off the task. Other top British acts, such as Oasis and Blur, had run up against resistance from the record-buying public in the States. All Saints had also found it hard to make headway because they were considered too old and sleazy-looking to win over the teen market. The fact that Natalie Appleton was a single mother had also damaged their cause with the notoriously prudish US public. Only the poppy, fluffy Spice Girls had managed to emulate their UK success across the Atlantic. The consolation for those who had money riding on Williams was that he wanted to make it there as much as they did. He was never going to be satisfied with his home market, Europe and an increasingly large part of the globe. For Williams, then as now, America was the Holy Grail. This was home to his heroes Frank Sinatra and Dean Martin, the biggest market on the planet, the final proof that you had made it, the ultimate ignominy for Gary Barlow and Nigel Martin-Smith. 'Barlow will top himself when I crack the States. I just know it,' Rob was prone to repeat as he prepared for the next trip Stateside.

In May, Rob embarked on a tour of Canada and the US to promote his newly released album *The Ego Has Landed*. The record, made for North American release only, was a compilation of the best bits of *Life Thru a Lens* and *I've Been Expecting You*. While in Britain and Europe Rob could expect to play regularly to 15,000 strong audiences, but here he was booked into small clubs holding no more than a couple of thousand as he tried to get himself noticed around the States. He was also lined up to do an exhausting round of TV appearances as the PR machine went into overdrive. MTV devoted an hour-long programme to him called *The Next Big Thing*. The highlight for Rob and his record label was getting the still relatively unknown singer on to CBS's hugely successful and influential *Late Show with David Letterman*. The appearance was pivotal in the strategy to turn Williams into a star on both sides of the Atlantic. But for once Rob's nerve let him down.

With his first guest spot on *Parkinson*, Rob had won over the audience and his host with his effortless natural charm and humour. His warm reception had been the result of a shared understanding between him and those seated out there the other side of the camera. They knew who he was. He was the lad with the smile and the laugh, the cheeky one.

They were aware of his chequered and troubled history, but they wanted to like him in spite of it. He knew them and instinctively how to play them. The task he had set himself in attempting to make it in America could not have been more vividly illustrated than on his appearance on Letterman's show. Rob sang "Millennium", the song chosen by his US label Capitol for his launch. But the expensively hired spin doctors and marketeers from top firm Nasty Little Man PR, who had convinced the network to book the livewire Brit bursting with pizzazz and personality, appeared to have over-sold their product if his performance for the American primetime public was anything to go by. When the pressure was on and he was sitting on the other side Letterman's famous desk, Rob's legendary charisma deserted him. Faltering and fawning in conversation with the world's top talk-show host, Rob appeared overawed and out of his depth. He began the interview with an awkward, gushing speech telling Letterman what an honour it was to be on his show and what a huge fan he was of his. His gags fell flat, his dad was a comic, but not a funny one, he said nervously. When Letterman showed a photo of a young Williams in Take That, Rob said, 'That's not me, that's my brother.' Letterman was so clueless as to Rob's identity that he believed him.

This has been the fundamental problem for Williams in his quest for the transatlantic fame he has always craved. So much of our interest in him is tied up in our collective history. He is part of ours, we are part of his. We saw at close quarters his disintegration, his rebirth and his ultimate triumph. We know his story. We were there in the confessional as he purged himself publicly of his sins. He has involved us, let us in to his confidence. When, on *Escapology*, he sings about being 'the world's most handsome man' we know that he was once a bloated pudding who couldn't even stand the sight of himself in the mirror. But what will his American audience make of this? The chances are they'll be thinking, 'This Limey sure is full of himself.' Likewise, when he sings 'It's hard to be humble when you're so fuckin' big', what does this mean to an audience who see him as anything but big? By the end of his first Letterman appearance, his host appeared to have developed a natural resistance to the Williams charm. Not bothering to mention by name the king of UK pop, Letterman took to referring to the 25-year-old Rob as 'the kid'.

Rob, back in the UK to collect two Ivor Novello songwriting awards, was in fighting mood. Those who were already writing off his chances of conquering America could 'Fuck off', he said. 'I'm in America and I'm going to make it and you're going to have to eat your words if you don't believe me.' "Millennium", however, failed to make the impression he was hoping for.

CHAPTER THIRTEEN
80,000 reasons to be miserable

The final guitar chord exploded out of the PA system and 80,000 people went crazy. Robbie Williams had taken his final bow, the band were filing off stage, hugging and waving to the fans. Rob, already out of sight of the huge crowd that had turned Dublin's Slane Castle into a scene resembling a cup final, had told the mass of humanity below him, 'Thank you for giving me the best night of my life.' It had been the biggest gig he had ever played. Rob had been on devastating form, cajoling, teasing the audience, sharing jokes – giving them what they came for. The consummate entertainer, he was the undisputed champion, the master of his craft. The critics knew it, the audience, who made the ground shake as they bounced in union and sang along to every word, knew it. But, away from the cameras and the smiling, lowly backstage boys grabbing a sly glance at the star as he marched back to his dressing room surrounded by his courtiers, the atmosphere had changed. Now there were no clench-fisted salutes, no blowing kisses to the ecstatic hordes, no wide-eyed scanning of the crowd taking it all in, no trademark smile. Now there were only tears and a feeling of emptiness. Later, the feelings would turn to anger, bitterness and self-loathing. How could he, Rob, the lad from Stoke, who wanted nothing more than to be famous, to entertain and be loved, go out in front of those people, who had showered him in affection, warmth and respect, and feel nothing? What was wrong with him? How could such unimaginable success, such unbridled adoration from his public, leave him so miserable? Just how screwed up does your life have to be for that to happen to you?

The back-slapping, the whooping from the band's dressing room, the glad-handing corporates, meant nothing to him. Out on that stage in front of the lights Rob would describe his overriding emotion as 'sad'. It is a popular word in the Williams lexicon of woe. Often he appears to be having the time of his life up there in front of the screaming fans. But as soon as he comes off stage his mood will change. 'Great gig,' a hanger-on or two will tell him. 'Nah, it wasn't happening tonight,' Rob is likely to reply. Even those used to being around the star can't guess which way he will go once he walks away from the lights down the stairs and back stage to his room. His dad, Pete, a man with a keen eye for a stellar performance, has often found himself congratulating his son on a great show for Rob to tell him he thought it was crap.

In the late summer of 1999, despite the phenomenal success of the Slane Castle gig and the rave reviews that went with it, Rob was ready to pack in all in, never do another show and never make another record. He had had enough and he wanted out. He'd try acting – anything – just not this. He no longer enjoyed getting up on stage and entertaining the public. The rush was gone, the drug-like euphoria didn't kick in like it used to. Those adoring faces looking up at him didn't do it for him any more. The loss of that joy tortured him. But the truth was that it could be 80,000 or eight standing there before him and he would have felt the same. At Slane Rob was in a state of near breakdown. Those around him feared, not only that he wouldn't be able to take to the stage for the gig, but, more importantly, that he was a real danger to himself. His behaviour backstage had been manic and strange. He was said to have put his hand on the thigh of a girl in his entourage and begun to squeeze until she was grimacing in pain. At that point he turned to her and said in barely concealed panic, 'I want some cocaine so much. I really crave it.' For most of the summer he had been in a pit of depression. America had been draining and ultimately unsuccessful. On his return from the States he had suffered a nervous breakdown. He didn't want to see anyone. He stayed at home, afraid to go out, frightened to talk to people, scared he couldn't have a conversation with someone in the street without them thinking him boring or stupid. He could not get out of bed or face the day ahead of him. 'I was even scared to go down to the deli because people would talk to me or look at me,' he remembers. 'And I knew I wouldn't have anything to say back to them. I thought I was boring.'

His desire to walk away from the business, from Robbie Williams, the cheeky, loveable pop star, had been fermenting since September the previous year when he released "Millennium" in the UK. Rob recalled, 'I wanted to give it up. I just thought, "I don't want to do this any more." I wanted to give up music and tread the boards.' Two months after the Slane Castle concert Rob was fed up. In the States again on yet another promotional tour, he complained, 'I have got to the point where I'm not arsed about what people think about me and I really have no point in being on stage. I don't know what I want to do, but it sure isn't this. It doesn't give me a thrill any more.' Of the spectacular Irish gig, he said, 'It was the biggest event I have ever done and I was so unhappy, so scared. It's that feeling of achieving what you have always wanted – the paradise syndrome. It's realizing that, no matter how successful you are, it doesn't make you a whole person. Where do you go from here? I had a breakdown and all sorts of nasty things were happening in my life and it brought me to that point. It was like, "Why do you want to sell yourself any more?" That's what I am coming to terms with.'

How can it be that, in the midst of such public adoration, with a sea of faces focusing on him, loving him, calling his name, he could feel only sadness, emptiness and suffering? How could such an outpouring of affection from thousands of people only there to see him leave him untouched, unwilling to repeat the exercise? The simple answer was, of course, that those people out there in the crowd screaming for him, worshipping him, meant nothing to him. What sad fools. How could they love a man who hated himself? What did they know, anyway? When you loathe yourself with such passion, with such undiluted disdain, how can you respect those who are deluded enough to believe you are something special? It's an age-old problem: how can you accept love until you feel you are worthy of it?

Despite his apparent readiness to call time on his pop

career, Rob was still managing at least to pull off the illusion that he was having a good time on stage. In October he did not so much steal the NetAid charity gig at Wembley stadium, as perform a smash and grab on the event, leaving such pop luminaries as David Bowie and George Michael in his wake. As well as signing a £2-million deal with Pepsi, he came top of a poll of *Cosmopolitan* readers who voted him the world's most gorgeous man. He even managed to be placed alongside Elvis Presley and Mozart in a survey of 600,000 people by HMV to name the top 20 musicians of the millennium.

Despite the enormous amounts of effort and money being expended on the task in hand, America was not giving up without a fight. His album *The Ego Has Landed* had failed to dent the Billboard chart and despite, or perhaps because of, his stateside stage shows, the branding of him as 'The Next Big Thing' seemed to be wide of the mark. In Atlanta, in October Rob had left an audience bemused when he walked on stage completely naked pretending to be lost. The stunt got him headlines in the UK, but was more Norman Wisdom than Jim Morrison. He had invested much in the venture and admitted, 'It'll be very embarrassing if I can't crack it there.' But the stress of the relentless campaign to win over the American audience was beginning to tell. He developed severe eczema, leaving his skin sore and red. Six months after the nervous breakdown he was still fighting a daily battle just to get out of bed in the morning. Even dates with the lovely Joely Richardson, the star of hit movie *101 Dalmatians,* failed to lift the gloom. They had arrived arm in arm at a *Vogue* magazine party in London in November and were said to have smooched later over dinner at The Ivy. But at the same time Rob was bemoaning his lot. 'I just want to lead a normal life, but the pressures are so great,' he said. 'Even my dog isn't helping matters because it messes on the carpet about ten times a day. I just wake up in the morning stressed and wanting normality.'

He was also aware, however, that he might not be any better off if he gave up his fame. 'With a personality like mine, it'd be much worse if I wasn't famous,' he said six months earlier. 'I'd be in some pub in Stoke-on-Trent, fat and moaning about how I could have made it as I collapsed under a table.'

To add to his worries, the row with American singer-songwriter Loudon Wainwright III had ended up in court. The singer issued a writ early in 2000 over William's song "Jesus in a Camper Van" from the eight-times platinum selling *I've Been Expecting You*. The row was centred on the almost identical lyrics in Wainwright's "I am the Way (New York Town)". In his song, Williams sings, 'Even the Son of God gets it hard sometimes, especially when he goes around saying "I am the way"'. In Wainwright's song, written 25 years earlier, he sang, 'Every Son of God gets a little hard luck sometime, especially when he goes round singing "he's the way"'. The two sides had failed to come to an agreement in August 1998 about sharing the royalties, and Wainwright's publishing company Ludlow Music Inc. issued a writ in the High Court for damages. The company also demanded the deletion of the song from Williams's album. It was estimated that the action was worth millions of pounds. The legal battle dragged on until February 2002 when damages were awarded to Ludlow

Music, who owned the rights to Loudon Wainwright's song and the tune that inspired it, Woody Guthrie's "I Am The Way", which was written in 1961. The publishing company had been seeking additional damages from Williams and Chambers, but the High Court in London rejected that claim. However, the judge, Mr Justice Pumfrey, ordered that "Jesus In A Camper Van" should be removed from *I've Been Expecting You*. He also ruled that 25 per cent of the royalties to the track must be handed over by Rob.

Rob sought to get over his immediate problems as the millennium was ushered in with a New Year's holiday in the ski resort of St Moritz with new girlfriend 26-year-old Tania Strecker, the presenter of Channel Four show *Naked Elvis*. The leggy Strecker, a single mother, was a well-known party girl and self-promoter, who was often to be seen emerging from nightclubs in varying states of high spirits. She was a former girlfriend of British movie director and future Mr Madonna, Guy Ritchie. The blonde TV wannabe was on his arm as Rob headed to Earl's Court in early March for the Brits. Rob, who jetted in from New York for the ceremony, ended the evening a record-breaker by adding two more Brits to his tally of nine. His number one song "She's the One" was voted Best Single and the video for the song, which featured Rob in Torvill and Dean mode on the ice rink, won Best Video. The awards took his total of Brits to two more than previous record-holder Annie Lennox. He had won five in two years to add to the four that he earned as part of Take That.

While collecting his gongs, Rob took the opportunity to go another round in his public sparring match with the Gallagher brothers. On stage he did a 'Mad for it' version of the Hokey Cokey imitating Liam's gurning style. Then he offered to put up £100,000 of his money if Liam would match the figure as a bet on a boxing match between the two of them. 'Are you going to do it or are you going to pussy out, you fucking wimp?' he taunted. The spat was the latest round in the high-profile slanging match that had won both sides much free publicity. Days before the awards, Liam's brother Noel had sneeringly described Williams as a 'fat dancer'. Rob responded by sending him a wreath via the offices of *The Sun* with the message, 'R.I.P. Heard your latest album. With deepest sympathy.' A riled Liam threatened to beat up his former Glastonbury chum.

Rob had already begun to formulate plans for a charitable trust to be set up using the £2 million he received from a Pepsi sponsorship deal. In May he launched the 'Give it Sum' trust, which would be run by Comic Relief. The cash raised would help UNICEF with the work Rob had become involved through his friend Ian Dury, who had lost his long battle with cancer a month earlier. Local charities in Stoke would be funded as well as 'Jeans for Genes', the charity founded to pay for research into inherited diseases.

Rob likes the word 'serenity'. It plays a major part in his life. It's about the way he feels when, for the moment at least, the insecurities, the fear and the constant lure of the bottle fade. Serenity is a feeling that Rob likes to hang on to. He even has the word as part of a tattoo on his arm 'Elvis, grant me serenity'. The same phrase is used as a prayer every night before he goes on stage. Band members, the crew and anyone hanging around in those cramped corridors backstage are expected to join the huddle while Reverend Williams leads the reading. The words, like the tattoo, are he says, for protection. The Catholic cross on his leg and the 'Born to be Mild' lion's head on his upper arm are protective too. He believes in their power, their quasi-religious meaning.

'Serene' was the word Rob used moments after boarding a frighteningly rudimentary Puma helicopter in the spring of 2000. Eyes clenched shut against the dust cloud thrown up by the rotor blades, he dived into his seat and surveyed the scene below as he was flown back to UNICEF headquarters in Maputo, Mozambique. Having taken over the role as ambassador for the charity following the death of Ian Dury, he had spent the day in the back of a pick-up truck being driven around the unmade roads of the country, which had been ravaged by devastating floods that killed 700 earlier that year, and the AIDS epidemic, which was infecting the same number every day. The trip had come at a difficult time. The weekend before jetting out to Africa, Rob had fallen off the wagon in spectacular style. He would claim he had been dry for nine months before succumbing to the temptation of another drink. He had been worried about the trip and his new role in the charity. 'I was petrified. I was representing UNICEF and I was guaranteed somewhere down the line to put my foot in it, which is always all right if I do it in my work.' It was clear that the officials, the government bigwigs, had no idea who their visitor in shorts and T-shirt was. Neither did the lines of pretty kids at the makeshift school Rob was taken to where classrooms were constructed from tents shipped by UNICEF from Kosovo. But, ever the entertainer, Rob was in his element, playing football and tag with the shrieking youngsters. The full impact of his part in the charity's work became clear to him when he was shown round a ward of toddlers dying of AIDS and kwashiorkor, a serious protein deficiency. Rob told the doctor on duty he had great admiration for his work and commitment. 'No,' replied the medic, 'You could do more than I ever will.'

Like his visit to Sri Lanka two years earlier, the trip allowed Rob to examine his own existence, his motivation and his desire for fame. 'I love a crowd, but I'm petrified of a one-on-one situation with people,' he said. He was aware that his craving for celebrity was the way of filling a void in his life. He was left with no one knowing who he really was. 'I'm left with Robert and I'm left with a scared 16-year-old kid that left Stoke-on-Trent,' he said. The brief anonymity he enjoyed in Africa was a welcome relief. Back home, Rob would admit he only had one friend, his boyhood pal and flatmate Jonathan Wilkes. His newly acquired £10 million fortune did not help. 'It's hard for me to find friends because, I'm 26, I've made a lot of money and I'm very well known,' he said. 'So I have to go to places that are exclusive and expensive just to protect myself.' Indeed the sheer difficulty of going out without being mobbed by fans or just bothered by streams of people coming over to his table in a restaurant was becoming a serious problem. Once, when Rob went to the races with Pete, a woman approached him and asked him if he could move to the left a bit so her friend could see him. That, and the risks that he would be offered drugs and tempted back to his old ways, meant that much of the time Rob would stay in watching the History Channel. The key to remaining sober was his commitment to Alcoholics

Anonymous and built in to his schedule, no matter where he was in the world, was time to attend meetings, often with the former addict, his manager David Enthoven. After the debacle of Rob's cancellation of the Europe tour the previous year, Enthoven had taken on the role of hand-holding mentor when Rob was away doing promotion or touring. He remains on hand to counsel his charge, play cards with him or accompany him to a 12-step programme meeting.

Both men would reap the rewards of Enthoven's Mother Theresa act. The financial gain to be had from a smooth-running tour is enormous. When, in the summer of 2000, tickets for Williams's UK tour went on sale, a record £6.7 million worth of tickets were sold in less than six hours. The tour, which would start in October at Birmingham's NEC, was an instant sell-out. The 44,000 seats for the NEC shows were sold by mid-morning on the first day of their sale. In Manchester phone lines were jammed as fans clamoured for the 75,000 tickets to his gigs at the city's Manchester Evening News arena.

Given Rob's problems with women, it was probably a wise move to keep the portly Enthoven around for emotional support. In April Rob had split with his manager's stepdaughter Tania Strecker. Later he would bemoan his luck with women. But it was his ex-fiancée Nicole Appleton who would bear the brunt of his barbed remarks. 'I've never been in love,' he declared in the early summer. 'Yeah, I was engaged, but in this crazy mixed-up world of showbiz, that doesn't mean anything really, does it? I don't want to go into the whys, wheres and whens because it's not for public consumption – it's about my inability to deal with reality.

I've not got anyone. It goes back to what Groucho Marx said, "I wouldn't want to be a member of any club that would have me as a member." And that's pretty much where I am with relationships at the minute.' He also made plain his verdict on many of the women he had dated. 'I think you know what they're after,' he said. 'Sure, there are a lot of people out there who want to be with me because of who I am but if I trust my intuition I'll be all right. If I don't, I'll let myself down.' His new, mainly booze-free existence helped, he claimed, 'Because of the new regime I am under I can now keep my trousers on. In the bad old days I thought I was supposed to sleep with lots of girls because I was a pop star. That's exactly what I did because it was handed to me on a plate every single night. In fact, there was too much of it and in the end it didn't make me happy. Unfortunately, the girls I've slept with have a habit of blabbing about it. As soon as they got out of bed they told the world. The difficulty is that the sort of girls who will come home and sleep with me, I can't have a conversation with. My love life is my own business and I am sick of it. After The Priory I knew I had to have a complete change of direction because my old life just led me to being miserable.'

That included his relationship with Nicole, claimed friends of the star. He had, they confided, nicknamed his paramour 'Nic the Nymph' over her insatiable appetite for sex. The energetic Ms Appleton had, he said, even refused to let him out of his house for a pint of milk during one particularly amorous weekend, which culminated with the singer missing a flight to Europe because he could not escape her lustful clutches. 'Nic wouldn't let me out of the door unless we shagged there and then in the hall. She had my trousers off before I could even answer,' the exhausted Williams had confessed. 'I wouldn't mind, but we'd done it four times the night before. I don't know if I can cope any more.' Was it coincidental that Rob's less-than-chivalrous remarks about his ex came as she was embarking on a relationship with his sworn and public enemy Liam Gallagher? The Oasis singer and Nicole had been friends for more than a year, but started on a love affair in the summer of 2000. Rob was furious over the relationship and broke off contact with Nicole as a result. He considered her liaison with the slack-jawed Mancunian to be the height of betrayal and to this day has never forgiven her for it.

CHAPTER FOURTEEN
straight talk

It is a peculiar and recurring ritual. You can guarantee that, when the drink is flowing and the room is full of tight white T-shirts, shaved heads and Abba devotees, the conversation will inevitably turn to the most crucial and pressing of debates. Gay men are, for some reason, more interested than most in the idea of celebrity, but their specialist subject, their starter for ten, is the field of in-the-closet celebrity. On any Friday or Saturday night you can put money on the same conversations being had in just about every gay bar in London. 'My ex had him, dear. Camp as Christmas he is, love. He might be married, sweetie, but he's in Shadow Lounge every Thursday night.' The accepted premise of these nocturnal forensic examinations is that the world is made up of two types of men: those who are gay and those who are gay but won't admit it. Somebody will swear they know somebody who has slept with a famous man who, hitherto, had appeared to be as straight as Jim Davidson. Top of the list is always Robbie Williams. The evidence for such definitive statements is, on even the most cursory of examinations, about as reliable as a character reference supplied by Neil Hamilton. But it raises the question: why is everyone so interested in Rob's sexuality?

The most likely answer is, because he wants us to be interested. If he doesn't, he's got a funny way of showing it. Witness the high camp performance with his flatmate Jonathan Wilkes during their duet at the *Swing When You're Winning* gig at the Royal Albert Hall, the references to the question of his sexuality in the lyrics of his songs and a chapter in his first official picture-led book entitled: 'Is Robbie Williams Gay'. The majority will ask what business is it of theirs if Rob is gay or straight. The answer is, because he has made it our business, whether we want to know or not. It's pretty unsurprising that he should find himself at the centre of a debate over his preferences. After all, here is a performer who once wore lycra vest and pants, knee pads and a baseball cap and was hired by a homosexual manager for a band targeted initially at the gay market. But why, since in the intervening years he has dated some of the most famous women in the country and brags schoolboy-like about his conquests, do the questions continue?

Robbie Williams is undeniably camp. It's part of his charm, a legacy of his music hall, cabaret heritage. It's part of his act, part of the reason little old ladies like him as much as teenagers. He trades on it and plays up to it. His first self-penned song, "Old Before I Die", set the tone. The hit includes the line 'Am I straight or gay?' The theme continues in "Kids", with Rob rapping, 'Press be asking, do I care for sodomy? I don't know, yeah, probably'. He likes us to question it, to try to work out if he is serious or just on another one of his wind-ups. The official line from Rob is that it is women who turn him on at the moment, but never say never. He will sing: 'I fuck arse, I fuck arse' over and over as a vocal warm up before going on stage, as documented in *Nobody Someday*, and then say: 'I have never slept with a man. I have never done anything with a man. The thought has passed my mind, but it always stops at his bits. You try everything once in life. I'm not discounting it, but it hasn't appealed enough for me to do it yet.' His record company likes the official line. Rob might not appear to care less what speculation there is about his private life, but EMI does. As the biggest star in the country, Williams appeals to both men and women, but at his gigs the guys are out-numbered six to one. Women love him: he's cool, handsome and sexy. The sexy bit is important. If a star like him were to come out and confess his homosexuality, would those same women still find him irresistible? Would they still be storming the crash barriers below the stage just to touch his hand at his concerts, would they still want to climb on to each other's shoulders to go topless and fling their bras at him? Music executives handling and promoting young male heart-throbs live in terror of the spontaneous gay confession or, worse, the outing of their money-spinning meal-tickets. We might live in politically correct times, but that hasn't helped George Michael's career since he asked more than the time of an undercover LAPD policeman in a Beverly Hills public toilet. Also, what happened to all the screaming girl fans after Boyzone singer Stephen Gately went to *The Sun* to tell his devastated groupies their dreams of getting intimate with him were never going to come true and that he was, in fact, in love with a man? It's all right if you look like Elton John, but if you trade on your handsome appearance and sexual attraction to women for a major part of your success, the gay thing is to be avoided like the plague.

The conspiracy theorists will also point to Rob's relationships with a series of famous women. He would later find himself at the centre of a furore over posed naked pictures of him and Rachel Hunter. Likewise, his relationship with ex-Spice Girl Geri Halliwell was open to question. The liaison between the two had stunt written all over it, a bit of positive spin for two stars with a track record for not being adverse to the odd bit of hyperbole when it comes to promoting themselves. His relationship with leggy TV presenter Tania Strecker has also raised eyebrows in a business addicted to gossip. She, it transpires, was the stepdaughter of his manager David Enthoven and has, in the past, described Rob as 'being part of the family'. When they started dating Tania was desperately trying to break into television. The publicity could not have harmed her chances.

The dilemma, more for the star's image-makers than for the man himself, is that the more you deny something, the more you fuel the rumours. That said, Rob doesn't seem exactly hell-bent on avoiding the issue. In early 2003 when he filmed a *Through the Keyhole*-style tour of his new LA home for MTV *Cribs*, he filled his living room with apparently gay men. And to crank up the campometer he went out shopping for a video the day before to give the scene added authenticity. When the camera finally followed Williams into the room for him to introduce his fey friends, the group of flamboyant young men were happily seated around the television watching that campest of classic musicals, *The Sound of Music.*

His relationship with Jonathan Wilkes, his flatmate and friend from Stoke whom he has known since he was nine, is also the subject of speculation. The gossips seem to forget that Wilkes does have a long-term girlfriend whom he plans to marry. Their rendition of "Me and my Shadow" was chock-full of end-of-pier campery, with Jonathan jokily telling his mate, 'I won't tell anyone you're gay.' The pair appear to enjoy the game, the sixth-form innuendo, the limp-wristed pantomime.

The singer does admit to one episode that dents his image as a love-hungry skirt-chaser. He confesses that he did once kiss a male friend in a nightclub. He says of the incident, 'I just walked in and there was a friend of mine there at the time and he came up and kissed me. I thought sod it, I'll kiss you, then. But in a manly way.' He described the scene as being of the 'lipstick lesbian' variety, fake homosexuality done for effect, to get a reaction from people.

But he does not rule out the possibility of a sexual relationship with a man. 'I might try it,' he admits. 'If I was attracted to a man then I'd do it, but as it stands I haven't been physically or emotionally attracted to a man to do anything sexual with them.' In the autumn of 2001 while in Australia he implied that, perhaps, his experimentation might have got further than that. Quizzed yet again about his sexual orientation by a journalist in Melbourne, he snapped, 'Look, I'm straight all right. Fucking hell. Tell the world. Sorry everyone, I tried being gay, but it just wasn't for me. If I could take a gay pill now, I would. But it's just not for me.'

He does, however, often state his liking for young women, preferably of the blonde and famous variety. Certainly, there has been no shortage of girls prepared to go into print and peddle their stories of sex with the heart-throb singer. What is Rob's reaction to these cheap sell-outs, the touting of private moments, the tawdry trading of intimacy? He seems surprisingly sanguine about the whole thing. The only time he has been moved to deny any kiss-and-tell claims was when, with mock anger, he told a *Top of the Pops* audience he was planning to sue one such get-rich-quick supposed conquest because she was so ugly he would never have slept with her. In fact, among those who trade in the field of kiss-and-tell revelation, there is an accepted rule of thumb that Robbie Williams will never complain about the disclosures of appropriately pretty girls. You won't find Robbie racing to the High Court on a Saturday night to tell some bleary-eyed, half-asleep judge that he needs to serve an injunction on the *News of the World* or the *Sunday People* because they plan to invade his privacy over next morning's cornflakes with breathless tales of his sexual athleticism.

As usual, with that most cherished of tabloid institutions, there is normally much less to a kiss-and-tell story than meets the eye. 'By now Robbie was keen to make as much disturbance in his bed as possible,' panted the *News of the World*. 'As he flexed every sinew, his Inoi symbol seemed to shimmer and move in the glow of the table lamps. Robin discovered she could make it move even more as she rubbed her fingers in his flesh.' The paper relieved the boggling of its readers' minds by reliably informing them that an Inoi is a Maori tribal prayer that Rob has tattooed on his shoulder.

'Raunchy Robin Reynolds, 27,' went on to describe in dizzying detail her 'three-day sex marathon' in Rob's suite at Auckland's five-star Somerset Grand Hotel. The blonde model, the paper told us, is the great, great, great grand-daughter of Rangihaerepo, the leader of the Maori Whakatohea tribe who was among Maori leaders who signed a treaty with Queen Victoria in 1840 establishing British rule over New Zealand. The history lesson over, we move on to biology. 'In bed he likes to give, even more than receive. He didn't have more than three hours sleep in three days', trilled Robin. The couple had met in July 2000 in the ground-floor bar of the New Zealand skyscraper after Williams had arrived in the country following an eleven-hour flight from Singapore. The statuesque Robin was having a glass of wine with her hairdresser friend Nicky when the singer came over to introduce himself. Minutes later Nicky was working her magic with comb and scissors in Rob's suite while the three chatted about relationships and Rob told the two girls about his exploits in a Californian Jacuzzi. Once she had finished his cut and blow, Nicky vanished, leaving Rob to invite Robin to come back in 30 minutes. When she did, she told the paper, Rob met her at the door in a fluffy bathrobe.

The predictable rock'n'roll bedroom drama takes an unex-pected turn with a scene, you suspect, never played out with Mick Jagger in the leading man role. As Robin entered the room, Rob told her, 'Oh, something's wrong.' The star was having a panic attack, he explained. Robin tried to calm the agitated singer down and then he led her into the bedroom, she revealed. 'I was wearing tight black trousers and a little black top, but he slipped them off, kissing all the time. Naturally, I responded. Then he told me his panic attack was over – but that was pretty obvious,' she simpered. 'He was very caring. All the sex we had was safe and he took care of that.' When it was time to leave, Rob, she told the paper, left her a CD with his London phone number on it. She gave him a cross made of New Zealand shell.

Robin fell into the arms of the *News of the World*, posed topless for the paper and spilled the beans on the brief encounter. But selling her story did not go down well in her politically correct hometown and Robin fled to London and LA to escape the public derision she was facing. Time and distance was to have a dramatic effect on her memory of the 'three-day sex marathon'. In hindsight, she admits, the encounter was not exactly the sexual equivalent of *Jeux sans Frontières*. 'He seemed very lonely, very troubled,' says the pneumatic blonde now. 'He asked me to stay the night, but to be honest, he just wanted some comfort. I sat on a chair and he put his head on my lap. I stroked his hair and he went to sleep. I felt sorry for him. I think he wanted someone to mother him. He needed nurturing. It wasn't a sexual thing.' Robin, though, did hold his hand while Rob had his granddad's name, Jack Farrell, tattooed on the inside of his wrists. When she left he wrote on the CD he gave her: 'To Rob, Thanx 4 looking after me'.

Robin says she had even asked the singer if he would mind if she told her story to a newspaper once he had left Auckland. Surprisingly, she says, Rob was all for the idea. 'He said he didn't mind at all, as long as I said nice things,' says Robin. So at ease was Rob over the issue, she says, that when she bumped into him nine months later in Los Angeles, he brushed off her apologies over her sexual revelations after their first meeting. Predictably, Robin went on to recount to the *News of the World* yet more lurid descriptions of Rob's sexual dynamism during her second encounter with him.

A little over a week after 'rampant Maori' Robin was on sleepover duty at Rob's Auckland suite, *The Sun's* front page headline screamed: 'Robbie and Geri: It's Love'. The paper revealed Williams and former Spice Girl Geri Halliwell were 'deeply in love'. The paper reported that the sweethearts had set off for a romantic holiday together in the South of France. An unnamed friend of Rob's was reported as saying. 'It's love. We haven't seen him like this for years.' The ensuing holiday in a £10,000-a-week villa rented by Geri was anything but relaxing. The whole break was conducted in front of the lenses of Press photographers. Geri, showing off her newly slim body in skimpy bikini, hanging around the neck of a muscled Rob and yelping in glee as he gave her a piggy-back on the St Tropez beach in front of the assembled media. Rob even invited the *Radio Times* to the villa to interview him during the 'holiday'. Geri, of course, is a past master at a bit of creative PR. The rules of the game followed by Press agents to the stars for pulling off a 'celebrity love-match' stunt are as follows: leak a story to a willing Press that boy star and girl star have been 'seeing each other'. Don't say they are in love, but whisper things about them 'never looking so happy', etc. Then, once the story is out, get the two willing stars together and make sure at least one photographer is there to capture the moment. Make sure your publicity-hungry clients don't give too many quotes. If they never admit the affair, they will have an alibi if they are later accused of faking the relationship. All things being equal, both parties will get a good few weeks of column inches before the sad announcement by their representatives that the relationship is over. They will remain friends, but it is, of course, 'a private matter'.

Throughout the month of wall-to-wall newspaper coverage of the story, Geri kept schtum. Rob, as usual, was more forthcoming. When face-to-face with the *Radio Times* writer Andrew Duncan during the trip, Rob confessed the relationship was strictly platonic. 'We haven't slept together or kissed,' he said, 'I like her an awful lot and don't want to ruin the friendship by it becoming more than that.' The reality was that the two supposed lovebirds had very separate bedrooms. 'If I had a daughter I wouldn't allow her to go out with the person I am, but I'd allow her to go out with the person I'm going to become,' Rob added. Then, while complaining about the ever-present paparazzi watching from the hills, the real reason for charade slipped out. 'Surely I'm allowed my privacy,' he explained to the journalist invited to crash his holiday. 'I want to jump naked into the pool and I have. A picture of that would have kept my single "Rock DJ" at number one for another week.'

The campaign worked a treat. Acres of newsprint were devoted to the couple with the story spawning a thousand women's magazine features, 'Can Geri really find love in the spotlight?' 'Why Geri will never tame love-hungry Robbie'. But there were those who suspected the couple had been stringing us along the whole time. Both were self-obsessed media whores content for a short-term merger to maximize

publicity potential. Geri, of course, had form in this department. Just under a year earlier she had been accused of
faking another relationship, this time with Virgin Radio DJ
and fellow ginger celebrity Chris Evans.

Twelve months later, Rob would admit that he hadn't had
a girlfriend for two years since he 'stepped out' with Tania
Strecker. But later, seemingly having forgotten his claims not
to have slept with Geri, he was changing tack again. As he
launched a PR blitz to promote his *Swing When You're
Winning* album, Rob was in apparently confessional mood.
He revealed he became scared of Geri when she started
playing with dolls and speaking like a 'psychotic child'.
Sleeping with the one-time Spice Girl 'wasn't really a sex
thing', he added. It would be months before Rob finally
came clean and admitted they had never had sex.

The 'are they, aren't they' tease was used again to spectacular effect during Rob's singing collaboration with Nicole
Kidman. The beautiful Hollywood film star, who had
recently separated from Tom Cruise, was persuaded by Rob's
management to duet with him on the classic "Somethin'
Stupid", originally a hit for Frank Sinatra and his daughter
Nancy. True to form, the raunchy video for the single was
not the only time, it was hinted, that the couple had got low
down and dirty. With the British Press salivating at the
prospect of the pairing of Britain's most lusted after male
pop singer and the Aussie superstar, the story went into overdrive. The couple were willing accomplices. They happily
played a game of cat and mouse with the tabloids with
reports of Rob leaving the lovely Miss Kidman's suite at the
Dorchester in the early hours. Predictably, while there was

the chance of a number one with the single, neither was denying the story that they had become an item. The reality, though, was less exciting. In truth, the relationship was never anything but strictly professional. Nicole gave away as much when, after filming the over-the-top video, she said in an interview, 'Robbie is a sweet soul'. Her description hardly implies the sexual fireworks the fans were led to believe continued after the video director shouted 'Cut'.

The music business is dirty. It's got more than its fair share of the get-rich-quick merchants, the barrow boys more happy holding a wedge of cash than a tune, the charmless hangers-on at the fringes, dealing in expletives and Ecstasy, the gangster rap phoneys with second-rate acts and second-hand Mercs. The old adage of 'where there's a hit there's a writ' has never been more apt. It's a world where you get shafted with a hug and a handshake. It's tin hats and every man for himself. The bottom line is money and never is the true nature of the business more apparent than when there is a row over it.

Rob's split with his first post-Take That manager, Kevin Kinsella, took the conventional industry route and threatened to end up court. The dispute was over how much money Kinsella claimed he was owed by Williams for the several months that the manager had stewardship of Rob's affairs. Kinsella, unlike most managers who charge a percentage of earnings, bills his clients for his time, a flat hourly rate for his expert services. When the relationship broke down between the two men, the subject of how much Kinsella wanted from Williams was the cause of bitter resentment between the two. Kinsella, who was once hailed as a second father by the star, quickly became a cause of anger and resentment. Within weeks of the official ending of their business relationship the writs were flying. Kinsella claimed he had a legal agreement with the singer guaranteeing him close to £400,000 in charges and costs. Rob's lawyers countered that there had been no formal contract between the pair. Kinsella claimed in court that he had evidence that he had sent the contract to Rob's mum Jan. The row dragged on and was heading for the High Court with Rob's lawyers Harbottle and Lewis preparing a lengthy defence against Kinsella's claims. His former manager was a further cause of irritation as he refused to take on a lawyer to fight his case and insisted on handling the action himself.

By the time Rob's debut album, *Life Thru a Lens,* was released, there was little love left to be lost between the one-time friends. In true Williams style he penned a sarcastic dedication to the Kinsella family, among others, on the sleeve notes of the record: 'You taught me so much about the business. I hope you get everything you want, but not from me!' he wrote. Unknown to Rob at the time, Kinsella was in even less forgiving mood than Rob had, at first, imagined. Kinsella had been busy preparing a 164-page document outlining his claim against the singer. It was to make very interesting reading. Today, Kinsella claims that sections of his statement were so contentious that the judge in the case instructed him to have them removed in a pre-trial meeting held in chambers. Kinsella made a series of serious accusations against his former client. Kinsella says that, after his departure from Take That, his ex-client was confused and troubled about his sexuality. 'He was very upset, very messed up,' says Kinsella. 'He was open with me about what he was feeling. He wanted to tell me because I think he was very mixed up in his head. He didn't make much attempt to hide the way he was feeling.'

Kinsella says that Rob himself seemed less than concerned about details of his alleged gay feelings becoming public. 'The problem in these cases is always the record companies,' says Kinsella. 'They were terrified of anything being written that Rob might be gay. It didn't fit in with their plans of how he should be marketed.' The confusion in his client's mind only added to the problems the young star was already facing, says the ex-manager. 'Rob was battling a very serious drink and drugs addiction. He had left Take That and was out on his own,' he says. 'He was under enormous pressure. He was terrified he was going to lose his career. He felt his whole life was going down the drain and he didn't know which way to turn. He was going through a very hard time, a breakdown and he was in a bad state. He just wanted to be able to talk to someone about it.'

Despite the many problems blighting his life, says Kinsella, Rob had no shortage of offers from beautiful girl fans. On one occasion at a Manchester party in the autumn of 1995 a pretty girl was making an obvious play for the heart-throb now newly liberated from the chaste Take That dogma. But, to the embarrassment of those in the star's party and the bemusement of the girl fan, Rob rejected her blatant offer of sex. 'This girl was all over him and making it obvious what she wanted,' says Kinsella. 'But Rob couldn't handle it. All of a sudden he burst into tears in front of everyone. He was saying to her, "I can't shag you. You remind me of my sister." It was very awkward for everyone.'

Kinsella's opinion is echoed by Ray Heffernan who met Rob at Christmas 1996 in Dublin and spent two weeks in his company. Heffernan says, 'I believe that at the time Rob's problem with homosexuality was one of his battles. He had been exposed to the gay scene early on in Take That. He hadn't resolved the issue of whether he was straight or gay when I met him. We would walk around Dublin all hours of the night just talking about his problems and the sexuality thing was definitely there. He was very open about it. It was hard for him to find exactly who was. The thing that he talked about a lot is that he always went for the most attractive girls as if to prove a point.'

Eventually Rob came to an out-of-court settlement with his former advisor. Kinsella says today that his opponent caved in. 'I was very happy with the outcome and what I got from the settlement,' he says. 'I don't think Rob or his lawyers were keen to go into court. I got what I felt I deserved.'

Gay jibes were also at the heart of the very public falling out between Rob and Noel and Liam Gallagher. Rob was famously branded 'queer' by Liam Gallagher at the 2000 Q magazine awards in London. When the Oasis singer stepped up to accept his band's award for best live act, he told the audience, which included Rob, 'This one's for Robbie as usual. He understands the letter Q.' Later, he explained the cryptic remark in typically pugnacious style, sneering: 'He deserved the Q Award for queer.' Kevin Kinsella says the brothers were uneasy with the constant, almost stalker-like attention they got from Williams after their first meeting at Glastonbury in the summer of 1995. 'Rob became almost obsessed with the Oasis boys,' he says. 'He was so in awe of them. He loved their music and their attitude. He followed them to Glastonbury and befriended them. They put up with him to start with, but he hung around them so much he became like a groupie. Noel and Liam started taking the piss, saying he was gay and fancied them. They are a couple of working class Mancunians and didn't know how to handle anything like that, so they got rid of him. That's why there has been so much bad blood between them since then'.

Rob is, of course, on a hiding to nothing. It's very difficult to defend yourself against gay tittle tattle. He has said that he feels it is insulting to his gay friends if he continually goes around denying he is homosexual, that somehow implied in his denials would be the assumption that to be attracted to men is something to be ashamed of. His approach to the issue seems to be the tried and tested policy of getting in there first, of pre-empting and defusing the nudge, nudge remarks with a wink of his own.

CHAPTER FIFTEEN
clean

The figure steadied himself, focused hard on the door at the far end of the room and with gritty determination edged forward. He moved with the measured, unhurried air of the drunk, self-consciously picking each step, planting each foot down hard in front of him. He appeared to have navigated his way successfully through the low-level chairs and tables until, suddenly, the floor seemed to move from under him. His body lurched sideways, his arms and legs, like a discarded puppet's, failed to react, so too did his face which retained its fixed, dreamy, half-smiling expression. His shoulder caught the side of a round-backed chair and he hit the floor hard. In the chic, fashionable surroundings of the members-only Soho House in London's Greek Street, staring is a definite no-no, very uncool. Most nights the plush club in the heart of theatreland plays host to the bright young things of British showbusiness, the see-and-be-seen brigade, the huggy, kissy uber-trendy set, the languid, cigarette-smoking cosmopolitan clones. You don't look at – or worse – point out celebrities in here. No, this is their sanctuary, where they come to escape life in the goldfish bowl of stardom. It's a place of refuge, a celebrity Nirvana.

Rob had received the usual Soho House reception that night and was studiously ignored by the cool clientele, but now as he sprawled noisily in front of them, they forget the house etiquette and gawped. In the summer of 2000 Rob had dropped into the club's bar for one drink. 'Just one,' he told himself as he was ushered beyond the imposing door. Two hours later he was hammered and moving between the tables asking for coke. However, he was out of luck. 'Fuck this,' he thought as he headed for the door. It was Soho after all. You can't move for drugs there.

All those AA meetings. The 'My name is Robert and I'm an alcoholic' mantra, the David Enthoven hand-holding had counted for nothing. Now, despite his previous declarations of a drug and drinks-free existence, Rob was back where he started – wrecked. With miraculous ineptitude he had failed that night to score in that commercial centre of the Columbian import–export business, but it wasn't for want of trying. The jungle drums were beating and the whispers from the in-crowd were that the new clean-living Mr Williams had relapsed in spectacular fashion. There were rumours of him bursting through the door of a smart Italian restaurant in the hip locality of Notting Hill. The room fell instantly silent, as the most famous pop star in the land, drunk and dishevelled, began asking the gobsmacked diners if they knew whose car was parked outside. 'Someone's done a poo on your Porsche,' he slurred.

By the autumn, his record company had gone into damage limitation mode and Rob was hastily dispatched to

Posh And Wrecked: Rob fell for The Honourable Jacqui Hamilton-Smith. The couple holidayed in Barbados, but Robbie was drinking and eating to excess.

Streckered Off: Rob dated leggy TV presenter Tania Strecker, the stepdaughter of his manager, but the affair fizzled out.

That's My Boyo: Robbie gives a Full Monty performance with Tom Jones at the 1998 Brits.

Doing It For The Kids: Robbie gets intimate on stage with Aussie pop princess Kylie Minogue.

Flower Child: Rob with girlfriend Nicole Appleton and her niece at a charity event.

She's The One: Rob planned marriage with Nicole, but their relationship broke down amid bitter recriminations.

Make Mine A Treble: Rob got drunk on free vodka but still scooped three awards at The Brits in 1999.

True Brit: Robbie collects two gongs at The Brits in 2000.

Waiting To Be Entertained: 80,000 fans at Dublin's
Slane Castle get ready for Robbie in August 1999.

Slane Pain: It was Robbie's biggest show to date, but on stage he was miserable.

Homeboys: Rob with flatmate and oldest friend Jonathan Wilkes.

Ginger Ringer: Robbie shared a holiday with ex-Spice Girl Geri Halliwell, but their relationship was branded a stunt.

Game Over: Rob and Rachel Hunter go on a date at an LA basketball game. The affair didn't last.

Reasons To Be Cheerful:
Robbie signs his £80m
record-breaking deal
with EMI.

the Caribbean with Guy Chambers. The official line was that he was 'exhausted and unwell' and was going on a private holiday. The real story was that Rob was over-indulging again. The danger signs had been there for months. In an interview with *Q* magazine that summer Rob had spelled out the perils he was facing as a recovering alcoholic. 'I don't drink socially, I know that much,' he said. 'I drink to get hammered and I do get hammered. I'm on my own when I'm out drinking because I can't communicate with anyone when I'm like that. Nothing spontaneous comes out of my mouth apart from "Have you got any cocaine?" Horrible, isn't it?' His bizarre description of how he wrote the song "Better Man" from his third album *Sing When You're Winning* also raised eyebrows. Williams claimed he prayed to the dead spirit of John Lennon and the murdered Beatle helped him write the tune. 'I sat outside with my guitar and I thought, "I'll just play to John Lennon and if he's listening maybe he'll give me something." Now that can be taken as arrogance or plain loony, but I started strumming these chords and the whole thing was written in an hour.' His battle with his cravings was increasingly evident. 'In a perfect world I'd never take drugs or drink again, but I have an illness,' he said. 'No, I'll tell you why I did it. It's fun. I want that fun feeling back and fear it won't return.'

His descent back into his addictions could not have come at a worse time for EMI. *Sing When You're Winning*, the title another barbed dig at his old enemy Gary Barlow, was released at the end of August 2000. He had also started a world tour with 21 British dates. In early November he had been so out of his head during the making of a video of his forthcoming single "Supreme" that filming had to be cut short. Then he had got himself into a fight at the MTV awards in Stockholm. At an EMI bash at the event he got into a slanging match with record producer Nellee Hooper. Hooper, the man who five years earlier had warned Williams's ex-manager Kevin Kinsella about his fears for the young star, had never been forgiven for his continuing friendship with the litigious Kinsella. As a result of the meeting Rob spent the rest of the evening drinking sambuca and had to be helped to bed.

Rob was hurriedly put on a flight to Barbados with his writing partner and checked into a suite at the exclusive Glitter Bay hotel. The record company's hope was that the steadying influence of Chambers would keep Rob out of further trouble. The huge European leg of Rob's *Sermon on the Mount* tour was due to begin after Christmas and a drugged-up, drinking Rob would be in grave danger of self-destructing under the pressure of months of touring. The Christmas period was spent with the singer desperately trying to win back the control in the war he was waging with his twin enemies.

As rehearsals for the tour started at the London Arena in Docklands, the sermon was read by Rob himself. With the zeal of the very recent convert, he announced to his band and crew that this would be his first tour free of drink or drugs. 'I don't know if you're aware that I have stopped drinking and taking drugs,' he told his grim-faced team. 'I know a lot of you have been around me when I have stopped only to see me start again. But this time I really don't want to. In confined spaces on planes or the tour bus, it is increasingly difficult to see you all pissed or doing what you do. I am an alcoholic and a drug addict and alcoholics and drug addicts want to drink and take drugs even though it kills them.' It would be that most un-rock'n'roll phenomenon, a dry tour. To ensure he was kept on the straight and narrow, his manager David Enthoven would be a constant companion, there to hold his hand day and night. The task of human sponge was nothing new to the one-time high-living hippie. He had become used to being woken by calls from Rob in the early hours. Rob would be having a panic attack or he was being bothered by fans ringing his doorbell. Enthoven would get out of bed and head round to Rob's place in Kensington Park Road to sit with him or take him home with him. Rob had, for several years, been increasingly the victim of panic attacks and had also developed claustro-phobia. The condition became so bad he once began feeling closed in while out for a walk in London's Hyde Park. The phone calls to his manager had become more frequent as Rob became convinced he could become the target of an assassin, a crazed fan in the mould of John Lennon's killer Mark Chapman or Barry George, the man who gunned down television presenter Jill Dando on her doorstep. Rob was used to having security men with him when he was out, but at home in Notting Hill he often found himself alone and scared. Enthoven is sanguine about the inconvenience, the constant nappy changing. 'It's about keeping the boss happy' is his public refrain. If Rob is content, the Robbie juggernaut rolls on, everyone makes money. If Rob is unhappy, it's likely the wheels are going to come off.

The singer's fears about his personal safety were realised in the early stages of the tour. At the end of February in Stuttgart at the city's Schleyerhalle, the show was in its final stages. As the band played the staccato riff to "Supreme", Rob, dressed in black and standing centre stage was halfway through the second verse. 'Yeah, are you questioning your size? Is there a tumour in your humour?' he was singing. Suddenly a small figure flashed from the back of the stage and raced to the front towards the audience. A split second later he was up behind the singer launching himself forward with both hands into Rob's back. Rob plunged six feet down into the pit below the stage followed by his attacker. For a few seconds the band, stunned by what they had witnessed, played on. Guitarist Fil Eisler was the first to abandon his instrument and jump down to aid the singer. Seconds later, the security team were dragging the attacker away as Rob lay in a heap on the other side of the crash barriers that separated stage and crowd. David Enthoven, who had witnessed the scene open-mouthed from his position at the side of the stage, was the first over to pull the star to his feet and Rob was helped back on stage. The band struck up "Supreme" again, but Rob wanted them to stop. 'Is everybody OK?' he asked the fans. 'Well, so am I,' he shouted back. 'And I'm not going to let any fucker get on stage and stop you having a good time.'

Rob had escaped with a bruised knee. Luckily, he would say later, he had landed on someone's head and they had broken his fall. The attacker had convinced himself the man standing out there on stage was not the real Robbie Williams, but a chimp-faced impostor stealing the real Robbie's act. He had somehow got backstage and out in front of the lights without being stopped. Rob might be all right this time, with only a sore leg to show for the monumental security balls-up, but it could have been much worse. His army-trained team of minders had seen their meticulously arranged safety cordon breached by a skinny German loony with a funny farm day pass and a grudge. 'What if he'd had a knife, like the guy who stabbed Monica Seles?' a tearful Rob told his manager. The incident only served to amplify Rob's fears about his safety. He decided that from now on he wanted round-the-clock security whether he was working or just at home. He had been deeply upset by the Jill Dando murder and the attack on George Harrison. They hadn't happened in America with its higher-than-average share of psychos. They took place in England and he, as the nation's biggest celebrity, was surely, he reasoned, in the gravest danger. The man chosen for the 24/7 task of taking care of Rob is Duncan 'Pompey' Wilkinson, a veteran of the Falklands War who was in charge of security the night of the debacle in Stuttgart. Now, wherever Rob is, Pompey is too. With Rob mainly in the States these days, so too is his minder.

Rob has confessed to the daily fear that he could become the latest celebrity victim of a stalker who takes their obsession with him to brutal extremes. But the fear goes beyond even Rob's description. 'He is obsessed with the idea that a nutter could be out there with a knife or gun, standing outside his house with the other fans, in the crowd outside a hotel. That's one of the reasons he has moved to the America where he is hardly known,' says someone close to him.

Rob returned to London via Paris and the Brits. He sang

his number one "Rock DJ", the song that earned him two Brits on the night for Best Single and Best Video. He also scooped the award for Best Male Artist. The award was presented to him by pseudo-squeeze Geri Halliwell, still milking the publicity fall-out from their South of France jaunt the previous summer. 'This winner is healthy, talented and, according to Press reports, giving me one,' she told the audience. 'So it's about time I returned the favour and gave him one – the winner is Robbie Williams.' The winner, sporting a fetching shade of eye-liner and, for the first time, a glass containing nothing stronger than mineral water, sat at an alcohol-free table and told his fellow guests, 'This year I will be sober and enjoy it more.' He was able to crack a joke about the attack the previous week, 'I'm sorry about the big security presence,' he said. 'It's not that I'm getting too big. It's just that people like to throw me off stage these days.' He also dedicated one of the awards to his five-month-old nephew Freddie, his sister Sally's baby son. 'Hopefully, your mum will show you this one day when you're older and you'll realize your uncle Robert was a star,' he said. Rob had not met his nephew until Freddie, born the previous October, was three months old. The awards ceremony heralded the arrival of a new Rob, sober and smiling. Gone was the demonic stare of previous Brit excesses, the wide-eyed speeches, the rambling dedications. This time Rob was in control and enjoying the feeling. 'Right now, I feel like the most loved person in the world,' he said, 'People have got nothing but smiles and hand shakes and "Nice one, Robbie" comments for me. I'm the luckiest geezer on the planet.'

His new-found sobriety had also given him a renewed

vigour for touring. When the *Sermon on the Mount* tour had kicked off the previous October, Rob had not been up for it. Still in the grip of his reliance on alcohol and cocaine, he felt no happiness out under the lights. The screams of 10,000 or 20,000 fans offered no remedy for the malaise, the joylessness of the experience. What he actually felt was loathing for the paying punters. What sort of half-wit would pay good money to come and see a useless prick like him? In the tormented Williams mind he was, while on stage, a fake, an overrated fraud playing at being the embodiment of rock cool. Up there was pop impostor Robbie Williams, the uncouth, brash egomaniac conning the public with his crappy patter and cheesy jokes. Rob hated everything about Robbie. Robbie was the 'charlatan' not fit to be in the same room as his peers like Elton John and Bono: 'I'm just not worthy of being around them,' he confessed. A couple of years earlier at the height of his drugs binges, he was invited to a party with the U2 singer. A nervous and intimidated Rob was so plastered that he stood mesmerized staring at a painting. Bono came over to ask him what he was doing. Rob replied, 'Bono, man. This fucking painting is incredible.' 'Robbie,' said the Irishman. 'That's the window.' The battle between the two very different sides of himself had left him exhausted and dejected. 'This doesn't really mean anything to me, any more,' he confided before going on stage in Birmingham at the start of the tour. Of being on stage he said, 'I've never enjoyed anything about it. I go on stage and beat myself up every night. I come off and I'm just sad.'

Four months on and Rob was reinvented – the showman loving the show, the fans, the business. But the Williams persona is unable or unwilling easily to throw off the cares of the world. His new-found joy at loving his work for the first time in years was itself a trigger for more regret and recrimination. Mid-way through the tour he had, for the first time, realized what a blessed existence he had. 'I'm so lucky to have everything I've got,' he said. But the reluctance to allow himself, even for a second, that moment of contentment, was sadly still in evidence. 'I've been walking around so miserable about life and the pressure of life,' he declared. 'And I feel so sorry for myself for having thought that way for so long. I just didn't see what a beautiful life I've got.' Even as he identified everything he had to be thankful, there, tapping him on the shoulder was the dark Williams second self, forbidding and wrecking the fleeting happiness, determined to spoil and sully that which is joyful, pleasurable. It is an utterly destructive force in his make-up, denying him the enjoyment his success has earned him the right to savour.

A legacy has also become the inability to sleep. By the spring of 2001, Rob was suffering with insomnia. Not able finally to nod off before daylight he would rarely rise before 2 p.m.

The idea was that after the *Sermon on the Mount* tour Rob would have some time off to recover from the rigours of being on the road before starting work on his fourth album for EMI. But in early 2001 Rob was approached by Richard Curtis, the writer behind *Four Weddings and a Funeral* and *Notting Hill* to sing a song for the soundtrack of his latest film, *Bridget Jones's Diary,* starring Renee Zellweger and Hugh Grant. The song would be the swing classic "Have You Met Miss Jones". Rob, a fan of Frank Sinatra, Dean Martin and Sammy Davis since he was a kid, jumped at the chance. In the spring when Rob was in LA to make a video for his version of "We Are The Champions", recorded with Queen for the soundtrack of the film *A Knight's Tale*, he was booked to sing the swing number on top chat host Jay Leno's nightly show. He returned to London and told his managers he wanted to record an album of swing standards and have the record out for Christmas. Clark and Enthoven's initial reaction was cool. EMI were even less keen. Where was the market for a 1950s revival record and what did this music mean to Rob's fans? But Williams had long possessed the clout to call the shots. If he wanted to do the record, no matter what the misgivings of the record company suits, it would be done.

Where else but in Los Angeles's Capitol Studios, where fifty years earlier Frank Sinatra himself had recorded some of his greatest work, would be fitting for the recording of *Swing When You're Winning?* Guy Chambers, again producing the record, brought in arranger Steve Sidwell to oversee the music and choice of musicians for the sessions. Rob, like a kid in a sweet shop, even fulfilled his dream of having some of the world's top swing musicians playing in the studio while he recorded, including Sinatra's own pianist Bill Miller, who at 83 accompanied Rob on "One For My Baby". Rob was on a high. The musicians may not have had a clue who the kid from England was. Steve Sidwell had hastily to introduce Rob to them when the singer walked into the studio and was ignored by the whole orchestra. But that first session, Rob said, was 'one of the happiest four hours of my life'. Predictably, the tears were hard on the heels of the happiness. 'I've been crying about it ever since,' he added. The record might well get slaughtered by the critics, Rob admitted, but the experience was a dream come true for a kid who would spend Sundays in the front room listening for hours to his dad's Rat Pack LPs, learning the words, practising the finger-clicking, the moves.

The record would be rushed out for the all-important Christmas market, but having only just finished a world tour, going back out on the road to promote it would be impossible. A one-off show was the only possibility and there could only be one venue that could do it justice – the Royal Albert Hall in London.

CHAPTER SIXTEEN
swinging for the lonely

It's like one of those Hollywood dream sequences. You know the type, where the kid with high hopes and a desire for stardom steps out on stage to rapturous applause, his name spelled out fifty feet high in neon behind him. He blows a kiss to the audience and begins to sing. This is, of course, the bit where the dirt poor sap wakes up and resumes his dismal life as pitiful nonentity. Not for Robbie Williams – his dream continues, Rob sliding twenty feet down a pole onto the stage of the Royal Albert Hall and launching into "Have You Met Miss Jones" while fans in evening dress go mental. There can be few moments, even in a career as stupendously successful as his, to match that high, the sheer mind-spinning intoxication of that pure uncut perfection. On that October night in 2001 there was only one thing missing. Not Francis Albert Sinatra himself; even Ol' Blue Eyes was there, sharing a beyond the grave duet with the young pretender on "It Was a Very Good Year". No, the man noticeable by his absence was the person who inspired the performance, Rob's dad, Pete.

It was Pete who had crooned those old standards at holiday camps at Perran Sands and Cayton Bay. It was Pete who had played those old records over and over to his boy, instilling in him the same love, the same reverence for the songs. Pete was the proud dad who took his chubby son to the open mike nights in Stoke for his lad to belt out "Every Time We Say Goodbye" to the pint-supping punters. Rob's mum was there at a table next to the Albert Hall stage, dressed up to the nines, beaming with pride at her boy. Even Rob's flatmate Jonathan Wilkes had his mum and dad along to watch their son share the spotlight for a song with the star turn. Pete, the entertainer the young Rob idolized and emulated, would have loved the night. This was his territory, the showgirls, the pizzazz, the tuxedoes and tiaras. What bigger buzz would there have been for a proud father than to watch his son going down a storm at the high altar of showbusiness, pulling off the audacious feat, pitting himself against Sinatra, Martin and Davis Jr and coming through? Or even Pete sharing the stage with Rob, like Jane Horrocks and US funnyman John Lovitz, joining his boy for one of the numbers that he could sing in his sleep? That evening was made for Pete Conway.

The closest Pete got was watching Rob's finest hour on the BBC. He did get a mention in the backstage footage, Rob telling the camera his dad was a big Sinatra fan and he had fallen in love with these old songs when he listened to his Pete's swing records. But out there where it mattered, Pete was missing. Jan was very much part of the show, being interviewed beforehand by the film crew, Rob pointing her out to the audience, saying 'Hello' to her as he launched into "Mack the Knife". Later, her tearful son finished the night with his triumphant version of "My Way" and shouted, 'Mum, this is your son singing. I love you' as a moist-eyed Jan mouthed a loving reply to her boy while the audience went mad.

It hadn't always been this way. Rob had shared a stage with Pete three years before, introducing his dad and doing Sinatra's "That's Life" together. 'I've been a big, big fan of this man all my life,' he told the crowd as he brought Pete on. Rob had also told TV viewers a few years before how he was still, even after all his success and fame, in awe of Pete, the consummate performer, the old hand who knew all the tricks. But the concert at the Albert Hall came in the middle of an estrangement between the two men that had lasted for more than two years. Rob had never been more visible, but he had vanished from his father's life. Contact was severed. Pete was out in the cold.

Pete Conway is a proud man, he is probably a bit stubborn too. They are character traits inherited by his only son. Pete made calls to Rob, but sometimes hit a wall of three or four people and never got further than his son's personal assistant, Josie Cliff. He is not the type of man to go down on his knees and beg. If Rob didn't want to speak to him or see him, that was just the way it would have to be. Rob knew where he was, he had Pete's number. He would be in touch when he was ready, Pete told his friends. Those who know the father and son are quick to point out Rob's volatility in all his personal relationships. Even his closest bond, with his mum, is often put to the test by her son's unpredictable moods. 'If you put Rob in an empty room he'd fall out with

himself,' says a family member. This breakdown of commu-
nications can be traced back to that day in 1977 when Pete
walked out on Jan and his three-year-old son. They might
have shared a relationship down the years, but Rob has never
got over that abandonment of not only himself, but also his
beloved mother. The separation also coincided with a period
when Rob was submitting himself to various therapists, most
of them determined to delve into his childhood to uncover
the reasons for his addictions and his many insecurities.

Their relationship had never been that of father and son
in the traditional sense, anyway. Pete was more often than
not living hundreds of miles away at the holiday camps he
worked in all over the country. Most of the time Rob spent
with his dad was in the school holidays when Rob stayed for
weeks at a time with his father. For Pete, never one to lay
down the law with his son, it was a combined role of father
and older pal.

But the issues at the heart of their relationship were never
resolved. Pete, the gagster, is genetically predisposed to run a
mile at the onset of anything 'deep'. With Pete, the past is
another country, seldom revisited except for a showbiz anec-
dote or funny tale filed away in the forensic mind of the
comic. He doesn't dwell on the bad bits, they're not part of
his act. The bad bits are a mainstay of Rob's act. He collects
and bottles them for future use. In "These Dreams" from *I've
Been Expecting You*, he tells of his mother's pain over Pete's
walk-out. 'She lies on the bed with her hands in her head
and she screams. He gets a kick out of losing the plot so it
seems' Rob sings. The lyrics continue, 'You never stopped
loving his misfortunate lazy ways. All the memories you

should have had are a cabaret haze'. The pain is a two-way street: Rob harbouring the resentment he feels over his father's departure, Pete having to listen to the bitter recriminations his son chooses to share with his audience. The words are hurtful, but Pete, ever the trooper, accepts the lambasting. 'That song is about me,' he says, 'Rob writes from the heart. There is always something underlying his songs, about Take That, Jan or me – whatever is going on in his head. With a lot of extremely talented people, as Rob is, things come out in them through emotion. You've got to feel deeply about something to write.' Pete, as befits his character, is determined to see the positives in the experience. 'On the one hand, Rob's background has been instrumental in him being as strong as he is. But his moments of self-doubt are probably brought about by the same thing. If I hadn't walked out he might not have had the problems he's had, but equally he might not have had the drive to become famous,' he says.

Pete, when he took time to spend examine the reasons for Rob's sudden dropping of him, concluded that his son, still in the grip of his addictions, was too ashamed to let his father see him in such a state. Nobody would blame him for indulging in a touch of self-deception. The reality of the situation was far from palatable. The nadir for Pete came in 2002 with the release of "My Culture", the song Rob recorded with One Giant Leap. The lyric, rapped by Rob, is a variation on the singer's early poem "Hello Sir", but this time transmuted into a stinging slap in the face to his father. 'Hello Dad, remember me?' spits Rob, 'I'm the man you thought I'd never be. I'm the boy who you reduced to tears. Dad, I've been lonely for 27 years. Yeah, that's right my name's Bob, I'm the one who landed the pop star's job. I'm the one who you told look, don't touch. I'm the kid who wouldn't amount to much'. These didn't, on the face of it at least, appear to be the words of a shame-faced son anxious not to lose the respect of a father he revered. In fact the song was an outpouring of opprobrium, a cold-blooded hatchet job, oozing with contempt, revelling in its get-even rancour. Rob was also hinting he was steering clear of the drinking sessions that had often defined the father and son relationship. 'I don't need a friend, I need a father,' he said. His words and his lyrics were a public kick in the teeth to Pete. It was not as though he could hide. Pete is famous in his hometown and beyond. Everyone who knows him knows he is Robbie Williams's dad. Even on a recent trip to New York, Pete was stopped on Fifth Avenue by a group of Brits who recognized him as the singer's father. Pete had to take the bucket-load of vitriol and live with it.

Pete admits he and Rob have had their share of problems. Even before their most recent separation, Pete confesses to previous breakdowns in their complicated relationship. 'Rob did go through a period of not being friends with me,' he says. 'I think this abandonment thing went through his mind. But I hadn't abandoned him. I have explained it to him and I think he understands, although he would have liked things to be different. So would I. Maybe I should have worked harder to have kept Rob right, knowing the effect that it did have on him.'

So, Pete was absent from the biggest night of his son's career. Seats for the one-off concert were priced at £175 each and one fan claimed to have spent £20,000 to buy his outside from a tout. It was certainly the hottest of hot tickets. Nicole Kidman and George Michael were in the audience for the best show in town. Perhaps the tickets for the seats behind Queen guitarist Brian May and his 'Mini-Me' wife Anita Dobson should have been marked 'Obstructed view'. Their hair, said a fellow concert-goer, had become fused in the middle, allowing no view whatsoever to the unfortunates placed to their rear. It was an untypical Robbie Williams audience, especially those in the expensive seats at the front. This was the twice-yearly up-from-the-shires contingent in rented dinner suits and Marks & Spencer's ball gowns. More Tie Rack than Rat Pack, they were interchangeable with the culture-on-a-stick merchants who religiously turn up to the Holland Park Opera every summer and complain that the music gets in the way of their picnic. But they loved Robbie. Rob might have been singing the oldies, but this was crooning Williams-style. The tone for the evening was set by Master of Ceremonies Rupert Everett, who told the crowd: 'You thought he was a thin boy band member who turned into a big fat slob in a rehab clinic … and you were right.' Rob, in front of a huge neon sign bearing his name, approached the fireman's pole that would take him down to the stage and chickened-out in a style more Frank Spencer than Frank Sinatra. 'There may be trouble ahead,' Rob sang before launching into "Let's Face the Music and Dance", 'but while there's music and moonlight and love and romance … let's get butt-naked and fucked up on drugs.'

Rob's tuxedo might have been expensively made, but the immaculate Sinatra would have turned in his grave at the sight of the one-inch gap above his tie exposing the top of his buttoned up shirt. Neither could you imagine the cool Dean Martin filling up as he blew kisses to his mum. He would have been more likely to appropriate the bourbon from the guests' table than the bottle of Evian Rob begged from one group of diners below the stage. When Rob removed his jacket as the show heated up, the audience were treated to the sight of his shirt coming out of the back of his trousers which were gradually travelling south as the evening progressed. The look was more post-wedding disco at a Dagenham community centre than Caesar's Palace. If the late Sinatra had been there in person and not just on film for his duet with Williams, he would have told his young English admirer to get a decent tailor and smarten himself up or he'd never make it in Vegas. Likewise, the Chairman of the Board and his crew didn't do camp. He would never have done a version of "Me and My Shadow" with Sammy Davis the way Rob performed it with bosom buddy Jonathan Wilkes. Their performance was shot through with fake homo-erotic naughtiness, with Wilkes teasing the star that he would let slip Williams's gay secret and Rob calling his flatmate a 'rentboy'. The fey compere, Everett, closed the evening by telling the cheering crowd: 'Despite whatever sexual orientation you came in the building with, would you get down on all fours and be royally shagged by Robbie Williams.'

If the whole effect was more gerbil than rat, it made no difference to the fans. They loved it. The following morning the *Daily Mail* declared: 'It could have been the most excruciating circus of karaoke of the decade. That it wasn't is a huge tribute to Robbie Williams's abundance of talent.'

Others were less generous. Simon Price in the *Independent on Sunday* wrote: 'Unfortunately for Robbie, Channel Four decided to screen *Pal Joey* this afternoon and when Robbie dedicates "The Lady is a Tramp" to his last three girlfriends, you can't help but picture Frank crooning "The Lady is a Tramp" to Kim Novak and shudder at the class chasm.' And music writer Gavin Martin declared: 'The lavish nature of the one-off event, complete with theatrical set pieces, dancing girls and walk-on parts from Jane Horrocks and American comedian John Lovitz, couldn't disguise the essential emptiness of Robbie's unspectacular interpretations.'

Instead of sharing the Albert Hall stage with his son, a 58-piece orchestra and a team of dancing girls dressed in Dior, Pete was watching the Wednesday edition of *Coronation Street* before donning his bow tie and dinner jacket in the tiny attic room that was his home at Warner Holiday's Thorsby Hall and preparing to perform his nightly act to the ageing holidaymakers, backed by two slightly homely-looking dancers and a lone keyboard player.

A year later, the two were not only divided by the rift, but also by 5,000 miles. Rob had left London for Los Angeles. He had accepted the fact that he had blamed his parents for his addictions and had allowed therapists to sell him the line that it was their fault. Even his relationship with Jan and Sally had suffered as a result, he admitted, but his sobriety had helped him mend fences. 'I used to try to think of my family and I felt like an orphan,' he said at the time, 'And now I do have that family back. I do have a parent. I'm not alone.' Tellingly and sadly for Pete, Rob was still using the word 'parent' in the singular. Pete was moving too. The times were changing. Pete was the old-timer surrounded by eager young entertainers who came cheaper. He decided to get out of Thorsby Hall before he was pushed by the new breed of entertainment managers who weren't even born when he was at his peak. His departure from the holiday camp coincided with the presence of a Channel Five camera team who were making a documentary about Williams senior. Pete, in his usual style, was playing down the breakdown in his relationship with Rob. 'Rob's very busy and so am I,' he told the TV team, 'He'll be in touch when he's ready.' Pete's friends interviewed by the film-makers were less sanguine about the state of affairs. They told of Pete's sorrow at being cut off by his son. The documentary team also benefited from a lucky fluke of timing. After more than two years of silence, Rob got in touch with his dad out of the blue. A delighted Pete was invited to fly out to New York to see his son. Not only that, Pete would be flown out on Concorde and was told by Rob not to bother packing. He would buy his dad a new wardrobe of clothes in the Big Apple. The only stipulation was that the Channel Five crew would not be able to follow Pete to the States or film him preparing to fly out. Pete, naturally keen not to jeopardize the promise of a renewed relationship with his son, was more than happy to agree. So keen was he to ensure that nothing would threaten the reunion, that he kept the news about Rob's offer of the jaunt secret from everyone, even his closest friends, for fear it would end up in a newspaper and appear to Rob that he had blabbed. So he was in for a shock when he read in *The Sun* the full details of the generous star's offer to his father, Concorde and all. Pete phoned his son, anxious to let Rob know he had not let the cat out of the bag. But who had leaked the information to the paper? Whoever it was, they certainly had very close access to the star. Only a tiny number of people at the very heart of the singer's entourage could possibly have known all the details of the planned trip.

It has never entered Pete Conway's head that those responsible for the star's image could have seen the opportunity to create some positive PR out of a potentially damaging TV programme outlining the rejection of a father by the nation's top pop star. However it had happened, Pete was happy to be back in his son's life. He was more than aware that Rob, the keen poker player, was holding all the cards. He didn't care how it had come about. The thaw in the relationship continued with Pete being invited to Rob's new £3.5 million Beverly Hills home at the end of 2002 – Pete spending the days by the pool reading or popping out for coffee with his son, Pete doing a double take as he realized he was standing next to actor Robin Williams in the queue. Such has been the rapprochement that Pete and Jan have spent a five-day period overlapping as guests at the Williams mansion. The former husband and wife even went out to dinner together while staying in LA. Rob also invited his dad up on stage with him when he returned to Britain to record *Top of the Pops*, hugging his father in front of the studio audience between takes. The relationship continues to thaw. After leaving his staff flat at Thorsby Hall, Pete lodged with a mate in Stoke. In the autumn of 2002 his home became a small room in a modest three-star hotel in the town. Rob splashed out £40,000 for an Andy Warhol original for Jan. Pete, on the other hand, religiously does the lottery and is sick of people asking him if Rob has shared his fortune with him. Rob's got a lot of overheads, he tells them. Anyway, he's not interested in his money. Pete has got it all worked out if ever his numbers do come up on a Saturday night. He won't tell a soul he's won. They'll just assume Rob has thrown some cash his way.

The *Swing When You're Winning* sideshow came at a welcome time for Rob. He was concerned about becoming stale and both he had his managers were acutely aware that he was in danger of, even by his own standards, becoming over-exposed. He announced: 'It's time to kill off Robbie Williams,' but not before the album of 1950s covers could be released in time for Christmas. The critics were divided. David Belcher in the *Glasgow Herald* was unimpressed. 'The laugh's on Robbie's effort,' he wrote, 'Instead of singing, what Robbie does is cobble together a bunch of gargling, declaiming and cod-American slurring. It's mannered. It's duff. It's no more than karaoke. Nowhere is this more painfully evident than on Robbie's much-vaunted 'duet' across the vale of death with Sinatra on "It Was a Very Good Year". What's happened is that Frank's voice has been scrubbed from a couple of verses of Gordon Jenning's classic arrangement, so Robbie can have a go behind Frank's back. The comparison is deadly.' But Neil Spencer in *The Observer* was kinder: 'The results go beyond high-class karaoke,' he declared. 'Behind all the celebrity hoopla, Williams has become quite a singer. Faced with an orchestra of pedigree musicians, he raised his game.' The fans seemed to agree and *Swing When You're Winning* sold two million copies in the first seven weeks of its release and went to number one. His single "Somethin' Stupid", a duet with Nicole Kidman, was the UK Christmas number one and the *Live at the Albert* topped the DVD charts.

While Rob announced he was having a year off in Los Angeles, his fans would have no time for withdrawal symptoms. In the New Year, *Nobody Someday*, the film shot on the *Sermon on the Mount* tour by documentary maker Brian Hill, was released. Hill, who had made a fly-on-the-wall television series *Sylvania Waters* about a dysfunctional Aussie family, was, he said after finishing the project, struck by the difference between Robbie Williams, the performer, and Rob, the man. He sold the idea of the tour diary to the star at Rob's flat in Notting Hill. To start with Rob had not been keen. Hill says: 'He turned to his PA in front of me and said, "Why are we having a meeting about a documentary? There are always cameras following me around." He hadn't even spoken to me at this point and he was saying this right in my earshot. But, when we spoke, I think he liked the fact that I was interested in the downside of what he does.' Never one to pass up the opportunity to unburden himself, Rob agreed to have the camera crew follow him on the upcoming tour. Hill noted that Williams was constantly surrounded by flunkies, PAs, security men and managers. 'What struck me was that he was never on his own,' he said.

What Hill captured in the several months that he and his crew followed Rob around, was an-on screen personality change so marked it was as if the Stuttgart nutter, who was so convinced the bloke claiming to be Robbie Williams was an impostor that he pushed him off the stage, might have spotted something the rest of us missed. Almost overnight, the singer, who starts off the tour bemoaning his existence and his horror of facing a hall full of people there to bestow their adoration on him, transforms into a limelight-loving, buzz junkie, relishing the experience of performing for his fans. The tour starts with Rob explaining the booze and drugs ban and telling his musicians and travelling crew that he didn't even want to do the tour. 'It's just a shame we have to go on stage,' he tells them. Rob was interviewed back-stage, in his hotel rooms, in bed at home in Notting Hill and on his tour bus. Hill and his team were given unlimited access. But the central question raised by the film remains unanswered by the end of it. How much of the angst-ridden, apparently painfully honest, Williams we see on camera is just another front, the showbiz creation of the consummate actor, whose make-believe character is so fused with his own that it's impossible to spot the joins? Are we being sold a fiction by the man who once said he was only himself when he was asleep? The alarm bells begin ringing early on when Williams tells Hill his reasons for agreeing to do the film. 'There is so much that is written about me that I am not in control of,' he tells him, 'And at this point in my life 99 per cent, if not 100 per cent, of what you see is me and if people don't like this then I'm fucked. There's no airs and graces. This is how I feel right now. I'm a bit boring and that's OK. I just wanted something out there that goes: This is it. This is what Robbie is.' It's the choice of the word 'Robbie' that makes you think. Robbie is not Rob. Robbie is the character he created with Nigel Martin-Smith in Manchester in 1990, the 24/7 showman, the always-on performer. Away from the business, Rob never refers to himself as 'Robbie'; that is who he is when he's at work. The other side of him, Robert Williams, is an altogether different person, given public protection by his huge alter ego. So just how much of the 'real Robbie Williams' that Hill promises at the start of the documentary are we really getting? Or does Hill's boast highlight the fundamental flaw in the film? If Robbie Williams isn't actually real, but an elaborate act, how real can any of what we see and hear be? Aren't we just seeing another stellar performance by a cynically developed and manufactured persona, bred for public consumption and put back in the lab when he's no longer needed?

At the start of the tour, which would take in 15 European cities, Rob is dreading the experience. Before his first night in Stockholm, he tells Hill: 'Whatever juice that gets you on stage, whether it is to be liked, to sing the songs you believe in or whether it's to make a lot of money – the juice is gone. And that's the scariest thing. I don't know if I am just burnt out. I have never enjoyed anything about it.' The definition of insanity, he says, is repeating the same thing over and over and expecting to get a different result. 'I know I am going to get on stage tonight and I am not going to enjoy it,' he sighs. He doesn't even like his songs any more, he confesses. "Let Me Entertain You" is a good song, but he's bored with it. "Old Before I Die" is crap, "Strong" is crap, too. 'I hate the chorus,' he says. 'I come off stage and I am just sad.' If he really isn't enjoying it, his undoubted acting talent is to the fore, as he bumps and grinds that night for the fans and whips the salivating Swedes into a frenzy. As the tour progresses, though, Rob seems nowhere nearer to enjoying it. 'I'm in no shape to get on stage,' he says before yet another show. 'There is the dreaded fear that they are going to get bored.' His mood is not improved after the gig. 'I just got sad on stage tonight,' he admits.

But there is a sudden and marked about turn. After coming off stage in Copenhagen, Williams exclaims: 'That was ace. It's ace being a pop star. There's no better job. I just failed to see all the great things about my life. I've never enjoyed touring before, but I don't want this one to stop.' In Rotterdam, he tells the audience they were his best ever. They had made a grown man cry, he gushes, 'I'm on stage going, "I'm ace" and 13,000 people are going, "We agree".' There seems to be no middle ground: Rob is a man of extremes. Undoubtedly, he was not relishing the thought of the tour at the beginning, but with Williams everything has to be either the end of the world or utterly blissful, there is no in between. His polemic is entertaining, but it does leave you wondering if the whole thing isn't just Acts One and Two of a production with Williams as screenwriter and leading man. How much less effective would the whole film have been without the drama of the tortured soul battling with his insecurities only to tame and ultimately conquer them? It's classic Hollywood happy ending stuff and far more entertaining than your average tour diary. And, let's not forget, Williams is nothing if not an entertainer. He treats us to his spoof of the demanding rock star, lambasting his tour manager Andy Franks for booking him into a smaller suite than the German Chancellor who is staying in the same hotel. Rob, pretending to measure tables that he has previously stipulated must be a minimum of two feet high, standing in his Jacuzzi and complaining there was no way he could fit five birds in there with him.

More absurd, but seemingly for real, is the sight of Rob's two highly trained security men going on a reconnaissance mission to a German sports field to make sure it is safe for the star and his entourage to turn up later for a game of football. The two, without a hint of irony, explaining to the camera their primary and secondary routes in and out and how they have timed the operation to the second. The film crew follows them as they cover all angles to make sure the paparazzi cannot bother their boss. In the end their endeavours are in vain. When Rob arrives, he decides he wants photographers to be allowed in to capture the kick-about.

The only thing lacking in the film so far had been a love interest. Rob, the clean-living, drugs-and-drink-free new man, playing children's card game Uno with his sycophantic band of hangers-on, was starting to look more like a monk than a rock star. The groupies were out in the cold, literally. They remained huddling on the hotel steps as the new version of the one-time bird bandit opted for an early night with nothing stronger than a cup of tea. 'I only get laid when I am drunk and I have slept with a lot of people, but I can only have a relationship with anyone if I'm sober. I will not accept anyone coming in and loving me and I wouldn't know how to love them because I'm a selfish, self-seeking, self-pitying fool,' he says smiling broadly. But later he has a change of heart. He has met a fan in the bar and taken her back to his room. 'I decided last night, fuck all this being nice and spiritual,' he says. 'I'm 27 and it's not illegal. I decided to have a shag and I did.' He pauses before adding ungallantly: 'And she was an absolute nutter.' In Hamburg he pulled another fan, he tells this film crew. They spent the night together in his room, but didn't have sex, he says. They were just kissing. But she was from 'Planet Fan' he jokes. She had asked him the following morning, 'But Robbie, what about us?'

Rob made it a hat trick of wins as Best Male Solo Artist at the Brits in February 2002, but was now firmly ensconced in LA amid rumours he was attending the world-famous Lee Strasberg acting school in the city as he planned to make a bid to launch an acting career. In April he renewed his temporary six months visa during a one-day whistlestop trip to London. He also put one of his Notting Hill homes on the market for £1.25 million. His sojourn in LA was now being referred to less as a holiday by the star and more as a permanent move. This was the place, he told his friends, where his children would be brought up. Rob had initially been staying in a suite at the trendy Sunset Marquis hotel in West Hollywood before moving into a rented house owned by actor Dan Ackroyd. There were other attractions as well as the weather. In the spring of 2002, Rob began dating Rod Stewart's ex-wife Rachel Hunter. He had been introduced to her children, nine-year-old Renée and Liam, seven, and Rob was said to get on well with the two youngsters. Rachel, said friends, was helping the singer keep off drink and drugs and had not touched alcohol since they began seeing each other. 'I'm not planning on coming back to England,' Rob told a friend, 'I came here to help me stay sober and it really is the best place for me.' He continued to attend Alcoholics Anonymous meetings in the city and was said to be 'joined at the hip' with the blonde Rachel. Rob himself was also waxing lyrical about his new girlfriend. 'She's gorgeous and a great comfort to me,' he said, 'We've been through a lot and talk about anything and everything. We've been seeing each other for a while. We're there for each other through thick and thin.'

The couple had, on the face of it, much in common. Like Rob, Rachel had fought a long battle with depression since the breakdown of her marriage to Stewart three years before. Also, like Rob, she had developed a taste for expensive sessions on the couches of high-rent therapists and had spoken of her need to 'find herself' after her split from her rock star husband. Around the time she met Williams she was telling of her continuing battle with her demons. 'I have reached rock bottom,' she said, 'I am as vulnerable and fragile as it is possible to be. I am shredded to the core. There have been days recently when I have not been able to leave the house.' Rachel conforms to a specific type of person Rob has surrounded himself with since his arrival in Los Angeles. They are often emotionally damaged or seeking answers in their lives. Many are those he has met through therapy or his Alcoholics Anonymous and Narcotics Anonymous meetings. In a town where seemingly everyone is being treated for something there is no shortage of young people, often from very rich backgrounds, who have succumbed to the excesses of the age. One such friend is Chris Brosnan, the 29-year-old son of James Bond actor Pierce Brosnan. Chris has a reputation as a reformed hell-raiser and once served three months in Wormwood Scrubs for drink driving. One recent visitor to Rob's house got into conversation with a young woman friend of Rob's, who, within seconds of the meeting, was confessing to a sustained period of therapy and dependency treatment. 'Do you like to drink?' she asked the visitor. When he said he did, she replied: 'Have you become so completely addicted to it that it has taken over your whole existence?'

CHAPTER SEVENTEEN
cupid stunts

Girlfriends, especially girlfriends of the famous variety, are good for business. The idea might not have suited Nigel Martin-Smith and his Take That doctrine, but ask any PR in the music biz and they'll tell you the same thing: girlfriends sell records. You might think that with an £80-million deal, sales of 20-odd million and a name that ranks alongside Hoover in the household stakes, that Robbie Williams could do without getting himself and his latest squeeze in the papers. You'd think he would be a bit bored by it, go for the Garboesque seclusion bit and keep himself to himself. It doesn't work like that and Rob's not alone here – they all want to be in the papers, no matter how big they are. From Madonna to Gareth Gates, they all crave it. There's hardly a celebrity who won't give you the hard luck story of their experience at the hands of the Press. And there's no doubt that when you're as big as Robbie Williams the level of interest you get from the Fourth Estate can be overwhelming.

Can you imagine living your life watched by a series of photographers who hang around outside your home the whole time and take the same picture of you coming down the steps of you house or getting in your car as many times a day as you care to repeat the exercise? It's not so bad in Los Angeles, where only the ex-pat paparazzi or the American photographers who regularly supply the British Press bother with him. Even so, Rob and his full-time bodyguard Pompey are on permanent look out for paparazzi. Rob, like most big stars, has developed a sixth sense about when photographers are around. You get to know the sound of the camera shutter, the glint of glass from the clump of trees, the van with darkened windows parked opposite the restaurant. It has become a game of cat and mouse and there are times when Rob gets off on the thrill of the chase. Turning out of the private estate on Mulholland Drive where he lives in LA, Rob will get a sense about the car doing a U-turn 100 yards up the road. Driving to the canyon where he walks his dogs, Rob gets his driver to slow down to see if the car behind will get up close or hang back. If it keeps its distance, you can put money on it being the paparazzi. If the guy tailgates you, starts flashing his lights and giving the finger out the window, you can be relatively certain you are just dealing with your average, ordinary Angelino road user. In the car park, Rob's driver will always do a circuit before his boss gets out. If there is a guy alone in his car and he doesn't have a dog, he'll be marked down especially if he avoids eye contact when the car gets up close. Rob knows the narrow, twisting roads around his home well enough to lose a tail or do a quick U-turn and block his pursuers in. He'll sometimes get out of the car with his bodyguard to ask the photographers to back off. 'I'm just walking my dogs, mate. Could you leave us alone?'

In early 2003 Rob was staying in New York's Mercer Hotel so he could appear on the bill of the Rock the Vote gig in the city and go to the after-show party at the Grammy Awards. The Mercer is a favourite with the stars. Not only is it trendy and expensive, but it also 'celebrity friendly'. It's the sort of place where celebrities go to meet other celebrities without being hassled by over-friendly staff, guests or the Press. In LA you go to the Hotel Bel Air or the Chateau Marmont, in New York it's the Mercer. It is so tuned in to its guests' desire for privacy that the windows of the hotel are frosted except for a small expanse of clear glass at the very top. During his stay in Manhattan, the city was victim to some of the worst blizzards in living memory. The singer and his entourage were snowed in and were passing the time sitting around chatting when Rob sensed movement out of the corner of his eye. A snapper was perched on the ledge outside with his camera pointing down into room. Pompey was dispatched to deal with the guy, a pap of the hard-nosed New York persuasion. Rob's bodyguard told the photographer to get down from the window ledge and get lost. 'Who are you, anyway?' said the sneering lensman. 'I'm the guy whose going to stick that camera up your arse,' came the bruiser's instant reply.

In London the situation is worse. True, the paparazzi don't generally try to get pictures of Rob from window ledges, but it's the sheer number of them that is the problem. They don't hang round in large groups on a day-to-day basis outside his home in Notting Hill, but there is almost always at least one guy armed with a camera who is prepared to sit there all day on the off-chance of getting a smudge of the country's most photographed pop star. The paparazzi tend to separate into two distinct groups. There is the smaller and select set who work on inside information, tip-offs from managers, PRs, restaurants or even the stars themselves, to turn up just in time to get a meaningful picture, something that is worth real money, like a picture of said star hand-in-hand and kissing a new girlfriend or boyfriend, or frolicking in the Caribbean surf. These are the guys who can earn £20,000 or £30,000 for a good picture of a big name. The second group is lower down the food chain. It includes a large number of London-based photographers, often with motor-bikes, who hang around outside the restaurants celebrities go to see and be seen in. Perennial favourite San Lorenzo in Knightsbridge or the trendy Nobu on Park Lane and newcomer Sketch in Mayfair are regularly served by several photographers gathered at the door in thick coats, scarves and woolly hats, waiting for Kylie or the latest *Pop Idol* or *Fame Academy* micro-star to pose for the flash guns.

Other B-team photographers prefer to hang around outside the homes of celebrities. Sometimes they are weekend wannabes of the quasi-stalker type who get off their jobs with the gas board at 5 p.m. on Friday and go out with camera and Vauxhall Astra to take out-of-focus pictures of the famous that never get used in the papers. It takes a certain type of personality to sit in a freezing cold car all day in the often vain hope that a star will walk out of his or her front door, get into their car and drive off, just like yesterday and the day before. Rob got so sick of photographers standing outside his west London home to take the same picture of him coming out of the gate, that he has taken to wearing a Robbie mask, which was made for the film *Rob by Nature*, every time he comes out. His reasoning is simple: the first couple of times they get pictures of him in the mask the papers will use them big. Robbie Williams walking around the streets in a mask of his own face is naturally going to have picture desks all over the country interested. But after the shot has been used a few times, nobody will be interested any more. It will just look like an old picture. The plan might be simple, but it is also flawed: it has not made the slightest difference to the numbers of dogged cameramen hanging around the upmarket streets of W11 when Rob's in town.

But like most stars, Rob's relationship with the Press is ambivalent. The problem for him and almost all other celebrities, for that matter, is that once you have turned on that media interest there is no turning it off. In a life that becomes about control, about snapping your fingers and getting what you want, about taking out a cigarette and having ten people rushing for their Zippos, the Press doesn't always play ball. For every saccharine, PR-inspired and manipulated piece by yet another tame writer from yet another glossy magazine, there will always be the journalist outside the public relations loop, who writes the stuff that makes the star apoplectic and the Press Officer at the record company have sleepless nights. Rob is prone to bitter rants at the media, but no matter how big he becomes he knows he will always need it. This contradiction in his approach is all too apparent. On the one hand, he'll rant about journalists questioning the motivation of the charity work of stars. 'Journalist wankers. What have they ever done?' On the other hand, even after signing his £80-million deal with EMI in the autumn of 2002, he was in an apprehensive mood before his 'comeback' gig at Pinewood Studios to give a first public airing of songs from his fifth album, *Escapology*. He'd been away for a year and other singers were out there, others had got in the papers more than him, he said.

That trusty sixth sense about the paparazzi had for once, it seemed, let him down. Rob, relaxing naked on a sun lounger in the grounds of a small, select and discreet Hollywood hotel, was in the mood for love. He was alone except for his new girlfriend, Rachel Hunter. The new lovers were wrapped up in each other. Oblivious to anything else going on around them, the couple were obviously getting carried away on that intoxicating first flush of love and lust. Rachel, topless and tanned, was on top of a clearly smitten Rob. Thankfully, given the circumstances, a towel just about covered his modesty as he groped and kissed the lovely model. The moment was passionate and private or so they thought. Very close to the lovers was a photographer, who fired off a series of highly intimate and highly intrusive shots of the lovebirds. Within days the pictures had been marketed by an agency that specializes in what, in newspaper parlance, is known as a 'property'. This particular 'property' was so explosive, so sexy, so jaw-droppingly hot that every red-top editor wanted it. As is so often the case when it comes to an auction of this type of tabloid gold dust, there is only one winner. The *News of the World* paid £120,000 for the world exclusive rights to the shots.

Nearly every news agency and celebrity photographer in LA had been after a shot of the couple. A few days earlier news had leaked out that Williams was dating the blonde Kiwi. To get the first shot of the lovers together would be worth tens of thousands to the guy who got the exclusive picture, even if they were only walking down the street or sitting outside Starbucks. In fact, after much ducking and diving, the couple were caught by a photographer when they had that most American of dates and went to an LA Lakers basketball game. This, of course, presented the *News of the World* with a dilemma. Having paid out a fortune for the pictures they were sitting on till Sunday, they were faced with someone else buying the first exclusive pictures of Robbie and Rachel together. Given that the second set of pictures were obviously far less exciting than those of the couple *in flagrante delicto*, the paper did not want to use the pictures, but needed to get them off the market. The final price, bumped up by mischievous counter-bidding from the *Sunday Mirror*, who were delighting in their rival's misfortune, was £80,000. So a cool £200,000 later, the *News of the World* ran its scoop on page one of the paper.

The pictures were certainly amazing, special enough for the *News of the World* to shell out an enormous amount of money for them, even by the standards of modern chequebook journalism. But, on the face of it, there seemed to be a major problem with the images. The manner in which they were taken, without the consent of the two people in them and on private property, was a clear breach of the guidelines of the Press Complaints Commission. The *Sunday People* had recently got into trouble and was forced to issue an apology when it used naked pictures of the Radio One DJ Sara Cox on holiday by her hotel pool. Why, given the obvious invasion of privacy, did neither Rob nor Rachel complain about their treatment at the hands of the hated paparazzi? Surely, this was a rare opportunity to get back at those who blighted his life and dogged his every move. This was after all the man who once said of photographers, 'Everywhere I go these days within 15 or 20 minutes the paparazzi will appear. I just want to get a baseball bat and smash their faces in.' Williams's publicist was unhelpful. 'Robbie will not be issuing any comment on the pictures. As far as I know, he is not angry,' was the official response. Rachel's spokeswoman, Claire Powell, was only slightly more forthcoming: 'I don't know anything about these pictures. I was shocked when I saw them,' she said. Why, also, for such a great set of exclusive snaps, did the photographer not have a byline, his or her name credited on them? A byline would guarantee kudos and make it easier for other publications around the world to know whom to contact to buy the rights to the highly marketable pictures.

On closer inspection, that was not the only problem with the pictures. For starters, they were just too good. Inevitably, when a photographer is far enough away from his subject not to be spotted, his pictures are, as a consequence, more grainy, more blurred, the result of long lens and fast exposure where even the slightest shake of the hands holding several pounds of glass and metal is evident in the finished image. It was obvious from the quality that the photographer was very close – close enough for the lovers, no matter how oblivious to the world around them, to have spotted him. The clincher, though, for those with the keenest eyesight, is the coffee mug next to the singer. This was not the exquisite china favoured by the sort of hotels that the richest celebrities go to for their trysts. This particular piece of china was emblazoned with the words 'Blues Brothers', the film that starred Dan Ackroyd and John Belushi. Was it by coincidence that Williams was, at that time, renting Ackroyd's home in the select hillside enclave of Mulholland Drive?

Neither the newspaper, the photo agency, Rob or Rachel was giving anything away in public. In private, though, to those closest to him, Rob has revealed that the exercise was staged and choreographed like one of his concerts, airbrushed, lit and made-up, the photographer directing his subjects like a sleazy shoot for a top-shelf mag. 'Lose the top Rachel. Yeah, great Rob, grab her breast. Legs a bit wider. Lovely.' Why, though, would a man so openly and blatantly antagonistic to the Press collude with such a ploy? Why would a star so hounded by photographers conspire to invade his own privacy in pictures that were tasteless, crude and tacky? What was in it for him? He certainly didn't need the money. Most, but not all the profits were paid to the malleable Miss Hunter, who so seamlessly fell into her new, albeit one-time, role as a tabloid soft-porn star. Rob's explanation to the few he has taken into his confidence is straightforward, if not altogether convincing. His justification went something like this: the Press knew I was seeing Rachel and every photographer wanted a picture of the two of us together. The pictures by the pool were so incredible that any other subsequent picture of the two of us would pale into insignificance and the newspapers wouldn't be interested. The photographers, knowing there was no longer a market for pictures of the two of us, would back off and leave us alone. There's a certain logic to the argument, but there is also a fundamental flaw in it. As we already know, there is no shortage of snappers, dogged or desperate enough to hang around to get a picture of a star as big as Williams, even if it looks like the one taken yesterday and the day before. Also, as someone well aware of the *modus operandi* of the paparazzi, he should have known that the whole point of the pap picture is the unguarded moment – the row between boyfriend and girlfriend in the street, the picture of them looking for rings in the jewellers or stepping out of the tattoo parlour where they have just sealed their union in ink. There would always be a market for these shots, no matter what had gone before.

What other motivation could he have had for the ruse? Wasn't Rob always telling us that he had moved to LA to get some privacy, so he could walk the streets without being constantly accosted by fans desperate for a picture or an autograph? The situation in Britain and Europe had got so bad that he literally could no longer do normal things like popping out for a coffee or pack of cigarettes, never mind going to a restaurant or bar. Why increase his profile with the US public by being photographed with a woman who, because of her marriage to an internationally renowned rock star, was very well known in the States? Surely that could do nothing to ensure the anonymity he professed to enjoy in America. Rachel was obviously up for it. She needs the publicity for her career as a model and her new calling as game show panellist and also because she has aspirations to get into acting. It could not harm her so publicly to display her obvious assets. The bulk of the £120,000 takings for the scam couldn't have hurt either.

The truth is that Rob also wanted the publicity. He had been away from his main market, the UK, for more than a year and it was time he got some big coverage in the papers, especially as he was trying to tie up a new record deal and preparing to release a new album. The shots of him with a world-renowned model and beauty would do no harm to his image as a red-blooded male and bird bandit, plus, importantly, the pictures would get him talked about in the States – a market, despite his many statements to the contrary, he is desperate to crack. Rod Stewart's intervention after the pictures were published was an unexpected gift to the Williams cause. By telling his ex-wife he didn't want their children to have to see pictures of their mother in such a compromising position, he fuelled the story and gave the relatively unknown Rob added publicity in the American Press. The blatantly sexual nature of the images would also, it was concluded within the Williams team, dampen down the perennial gay rumours about their star.

But, given Rob's admission that the whole thing was a set-up, his decision to pose for the pictures is looking increasingly like a PR mistake – the sort of ill-judged, badly timed, cheap trick that ends up tainting everyone involved, but more particularly Rob himself. It leaves him wide open to the accusation that, if he staged the pictures, how do we know he didn't stage the whole 'affair' with his willing accomplice? And if he needs to manufacture relationships with women, what is it he trying to hide about the nature of his sexuality?

CHAPTER EIGHTEEN
the £80 million year off

In the pink sunshine of a warm late afternoon a large four-wheel-drive SUV trundled the length of a long driveway in first gear until it reached an impressive set of gates. The vehicle performed a U-turn and slowly returned to the imposing house at the other end. The car repeated the manoeuvre several times.

In the opulent surroundings of their Regent's Park offices, the bean-counters and number-crunchers were checking their sums. Their calculations were complicated and exhaustive, checked and re-checked. They had to be. They would form the basis for the biggest-ever music deal in British history. In a few hours executives from EMI would make the formal offer of £80 million to secure the services of one Robbie Williams.

If Rob was feeling the pressure of the wait while his managers and lawyers argued about the fine detail of the deal with the record label, he wasn't showing it. Shades on, he swung the car round again, put in into drive, listened to the engine growl, then began the trawl to the gates at the end of his drive again. He doesn't go beyond them, not alone anyway, and not at the wheel. He has never passed his driving test and, anyway, he would always feel more comfortable with his bodyguard Pomp behind the controls. It's just that sometimes, when there is nothing better to do, he jumps in the car and does a few circuits of the gated estate where he lives on Los Angeles's Mulholland Drive. It's not exactly Route 66 wind in the hair, joy of the open road stuff, but Rob enjoys it anyway.

If you're going to have a year off it always makes sense to spend some of it, at least, knocking out a few tracks for a new album that will get the biggest and richest record companies in the world banging down your door with suitcases full of cash. It all depends, of course, on your definition of time off. At the beginning of 2002, Rob's people were telling all interested parties that Rob would be staying in his new home city of LA. He had decided, unilaterally, that he needed a complete break from the music business, from the pressures and stresses of being the most bankable name in European music. The previous year, dominated as it was by touring the world, had taken its toll on the singer. He would spend some time in the sun with the new-found friends he had met in Hollywood and just chill for a bit. He deserved the break. He didn't exactly go to ground. Instead of seeing him strutting his stuff in his usual territory before the lights on stage, his fans would have to get their Robbie fix with pictures of their hero hanging out at LA coffee bars or the odd shot of him walking his three dogs, Sam, Rudy and Sid, at Runyon Canyon. The record company no longer had a say in how he spent his time. His deal with EMI had come to an end when he presented them with the surprise package that was *Swing*

When You're Winning. Rob was a free agent again and it would be up to him when he went back to work.

It doesn't really matter how much you've got in the bank. If you are driven by a desire for success, that dull ache always there, forcing, propelling you on, you never really give yourself the option of resting on your laurels. Rob, as astute as any in the fickle ways and wants of the music-buying public, was never going to allow himself to sit back for long. Anyway, despite the tormented, reluctant angst-ridden bit, he actually enjoys it. The fiercely competitive streak is there. No pretty boy with a winning smile and a good producer is going to knock him of his perch, wrestle the throne from him, not yet at least. There's no sitting back in this business. There's a fine line between a timely return to a public suffering from withdrawal and eager for more, and staying away too long and becoming history. Rob would not make that mistake. Besides, this was never going to be simply a case of just maintaining, of hanging on to the territory he had made his. No, the plan with Williams has always been to push on, to win new markets, to make it bigger and better. That would be the whole point of that two-inch thick contract when he signed his name on it in the early autumn of the year. Rob had promised EMI America. If he couldn't deliver that particular Holy Grail, he would have – by his own standards at least – failed. Publicly, he talks down the pressure he is under. Cracking America means nothing to him. He couldn't give a shit. He doesn't want to commit to the mammoth slog that is involved in winning over that huge continent. He likes the idea of having at least one part of the world where he can be anonymous, where he can find out who he is and meet people who haven't only previously seen him in two dimensions. He nearly pulls it off, but Rob is undoubtedly a good actor. The truth is different. When the germ of *Escapology* was forming in his mind, it had USA written through it like a stick of rock.

This time the album would be made using Rob's money. With the EMI deal over, Rob knew he could sign on with any number of eager suitors immediately. But he decided to make his next album first, have it in the can and give the big hitters a listen to the finished product before breaking to them the number of noughts he expected there to be on any offer they made him. Much of the writing was already done. Rob and Guy Chambers had many a dull day on the road to throw ideas around and Rob had been stockpiling new material since *Sing When You're Winning* was finished two years earlier. By the summer, Rob, Guy and co-producer Steve Power were laying down the tracks in three LA studios that would make up his fourth album of new material. Rob, now clean, had dispensed with the bottle of vodka under the mixing desk, but still felt the need to lighten up the often dreary proceedings in the studio. One day he arrived at the studio in full Superman costume, complete with artificially inflated chest and biceps. Another time he told the technicians on the other side of the glass screen that he wanted the lights out to add more atmosphere to his singing take. When the studio was once again illuminated, Rob was standing stark naked in the recording booth.

Meanwhile Tim Clark and David Enthoven would be responsible for getting the bidders together. There was also a Plan B. If the money was not right, Rob would put the record out himself, fund it and promote it out of his own pocket and have a label, most probably old record company EMI, distribute it. It was a bold strategy. London media consultants Equinox were hired to offer advice on the project if Rob and his people decided to take the highly unusual course and go it alone. CD manufacturers and retailers were also contacted. The move was a clever one, it added even more muscle to his management team's bargaining power when it came to talking cold, hard cash with the record companies' men in suits.

EMI was desperate to renew their incredibly successful relationship with the singer they had taken on as a jabbering drunk six years earlier. But there were others in the frame as well. Universal boss Lucian Grainge was talking big. He would, he said, give Rob 'anything he wants' to sign with his label. Richard Branson was also bidding to pull off the music business transfer of the decade. As it was, Branson's V2 label, partly owned by merchant bank Morgan Grenfell, dropped out of the bidding when it reached £25 million. It would go more than three times higher into the thin air at the very peak of the pop world before EMI and its record label boss Alain Levy were able to wrestle back their biggest talent and money-spinner from the jaws of their slavering rivals.

The deal, announced at IE's Shepherd's Bush offices, was given the added gloss of some impromptu Robbie Williams theatre. Standing outside in front of the Press and TV camera crews, Rob was giving another killer performance. 'I'm rich beyond my wildest dreams,' he yelled with soundbite savvy. Asked if the deal was really worth £80 million, he joked: 'My mum said it would be really uncouth of me to talk about money … I'm going back now to count it all.' It was classic Williams. There was none of the fake nonchalance of the cool corporate rockers. None of that 'it's not about money, it's about artistic freedom' crap. It might have been scripted, but it felt real. It was the sort of reaction you'd expect from a kid from Stoke whose every ship had come in all at the same time. Only Williams could be crowned the biggest player in a billion dollar business and pull off the self-deprecation. OK, he was mega-rich, but he is still scared of his mum. He wasn't the Son of God, he was a very naughty boy.

The deal, twice the previous UK record negotiated for Elton John, was, nonetheless, a gamble for the label. The company had spectacularly burnt its fingers with the $70 million five-album deal they signed with US mega-warbler Mariah Carey. EMI were forced to pay $20 million to buy themselves out of the deal when Carey's first record for them, *Glitter*, bombed. The debacle had cost EMI boss Ken Berry his job and left the company twitchy about repeating the mistake. They would want a lot for their money. On top of CD sales, they would also profit from videos, tour receipts, merchandising and Rob's back catalogue. Moreover, Rob would not receive the £80 million up front. He would initially get a signing-on fee of £10 million plus a further £15 million advance against sales for the first album of the deal, *Escapology*. The rest would be split between the remaining albums he was contracted to produce for his bosses. But, written into the contract, was the agreement that if the first album failed to reach the targets set for it, the remaining payments would shrink. Without continued success, Rob would see less of the £80 million than he might have imagined. In fact, analysts were convinced that factored into the deal had to be the understanding that Rob would have to make significant inroads into the US market in order to see anything like the sums that were being bandied around. *Escapology*, a collection of songs so blatantly aimed at the huge American AOR market, would become instantly known in the business as the '£80 million record'. If it did the business for him Stateside, Rob would almost guarantee cashing in to such a huge degree. If not, the odds on him raking in anything like that amount were slim, to say the least. Not everyone was convinced that EMI's sums were correct. Following the announcement of the deal EMI's share price closed down 1.75 pence.

A further complication for EMI was the news, revealed immediately after the deal was signed, that Rob had split from his writing partner Guy Chambers. The two men had achieved phenomenal success with their five-year collaboration and it was Chambers who had been credited with being the musical driving force behind Williams's career. But in the final months of their partnership, their personal relationship had begun to sour. Always very different characters, Chambers, the middle-class music-school boy, had developed a taste for fine wine and food and had gained the nickname 'The Lord'. Like Williams, Guy, a hard-up, struggling songwriter and musician when he they met, had become a millionaire many times over as a result of their association. Those who know him point out he is keenly aware of his own talent and not averse to pushing home the point of how important he has been in the regeneration of the once washed-up Williams. Privately, Chambers, the serious musician had tired of Rob's loudmouth antics and japes while recording. He would complain about Rob's habit of shrieking, yelping and whooping for no apparent reason into the microphone while they were laying down tracks, leaving the headphone-wearing producer wincing in pain. Significantly, too, Rob's attitude to writing and recording had changed. Once content to let Guy and Steve Power 'do all the work', he was increasingly ready to offer not only an opinion, but often an instruction about how things should be done. *Swing When You're Winning* had been a turning point. If there was ever a doubt in his mind that his success was fundamentally due, not only to the songs he had been producing with Chambers, but to his sheer dynamism as a performer, it had been removed with that highly successful project. Not only that, Rob was finding his feet as a complete songwriter. No longer content just to write lyrics and have Guy turn them into songs, he was trying his hand at writing the music as well with the help of the chords he had been learning on the guitar.

In the winter of 2001, while on tour in Europe, Rob was spending more time writing and often without the previously ubiquitous Chambers. In his hotel room one night after a gig, Rob was trying to work out the chords to the Beatles song "Norwegian Wood". What came out was the basis for the first song he would complete himself. "Nan's Song", a heartfelt tribute to his dead grandmother, would eventually appear on *Escapology* as would another song written without the help of Chambers, "Come Undone". Guy was also in demand elsewhere. Other stars were keen to make use of some of his undoubted chart gold-dust and he was being made attractive offers, not least by Britney Spears. Writing a hit for the Princess of Pop would guarantee a worldwide audience for his work and, most important of all, an entrée to the previously off-limits US charts. In the final analysis, it was that perennial music business issue of money that would drive the two men apart. Rob wanted to continue the relationship, but the new EMI deal had ratcheted things up. Guy, as 50 per cent of Britain's most successful songwriting partnership, would want his cut from the crock of gold. He also wanted to devote more time to making an album of his own material and was also developing an all-girl group, The Licks, who he had signed to his own label Orgasmatron. By the beginning of October, as the deal with EMI deal was being finalized, negotiations between Williams and Chambers had stalled. Rob, fired up by his new role as the undisputed King of Pop told his advisors: 'I won't be held to ransom. If Guy doesn't like it, he can fuck off.' Guy was incandescent when word got back to him that Rob had begun referring to him as 'just another employee'. It was the final straw. Two years earlier, Rob had dedicated *Sing When You're Winning*, 'To Guy Chambers who is as much Robbie Williams as I am.' Now the situation had changed: clean and focused, Rob was the master of his own destiny. With more power than ever before, he was in no mood to be dictated to. He was also keen to work with other songwriters and, let's face it, he knew the best would want to work with a singer who was well on his way to shifting 25 million records.

Guy was playing down the rift. 'I am obviously very proud of what Robbie and I have achieved, but I feel it is time to move on and spread my wings a bit,' he said. 'I want to work with other people and try my hand at other areas of the industry. There is only so long you can keep doing the same thing without becoming complacent and it's time for me to try new challenges.' To start with, Rob, too, was appearing to be circumspect. 'My partnership with Guy, unfortunately, for the foreseeable future, has come to an end. I don't want to get into it. It would embarrass him and it would embarrass myself. But I can categorically say I never once asked for an exclusivity deal with Guy,' he said. But time is not a healer for Williams. Instead, it allows old differences to fester and intensify. By the time he was showcasing his new album to an invited audience for a TV special at Pinewood Studios at the end of October, he was implying he had given Chambers the push. 'We have had a redundancy in the band,' he told the fans. A month later when asked about the split, he refused to talk about it, then raised his glass to cover his mouth, affected a different accent and said: 'He's a man who wanted too much money.'

In November of 2002 *Escapology* was released in the UK along with the first single "Feel". By Christmas the album had been number one for five weeks and had sold 1.2 million copies in Britain alone. The single, with a video filmed in Canada and featuring actress Daryl Hannah, would only make a disappointing number four. Rob was feeling the weight of the massive new deal with EMI. He had been almost a year away from a stage and, like a record-breaking football signing, he was under pressure to perform. *Escapology* would herald a new era for Rob. "Nan's Song" and "Come Undone" were the first songs completed without the writing input of Guy Chambers. Unwittingly, the songs became a statement of intent, proof or otherwise that Rob could manage without his partner. Once the announcement was made that the multi-platinum winning collaboration between the two men was over, those songs became the ones by which the next stage of his career would be judged. The question was, did Rob have a future as a writer without Chambers? The answer was yes and no. "Come Undone", a four-way collaboration and the second single to be released from the album, is a brutal and damning self-assessment. He sings: 'So impressed, but so in awe. Such a saint, but such a whore.' On the face of it, the song is a no-holds-barred analysis of the contradictions at work in the Williams persona, but it is more accurately described as a letter of apology to those close to him who suffered at the hands of his addictions. Anthemic and raw, it is one of his most powerful and honest creations. It also has him doing an uncanny impersonation of Jon Bon Jovi at the end, although you can't really imagine the one-time poodle-permed soft rocker screaming 'I am scum'.

Williams is understandably proud of "Nan's Song". It is the first track he wrote by himself, words and music, figuring out the chords on his guitar as he went. He wanted this first song to be about someone he loved. His grandmother Betty Williams was incredibly close to her grandson. It was Betty who would pick him up from school while Jan worked. Rob spent as much time in her terraced home in Stoke as he did his own. She was protective of him. She didn't even like him playing outside with the other kids because she worried about him. When she died Rob was in the midst of his addiction to alcohol and drugs. Her death hit him very hard. So "Nan's Song" is a very personal to Williams. You just wish he'd have kept it that way, then we wouldn't be forced to have an opinion about it. But, because he chose to put the song on his album, we are. The comparison with the other offerings on the record is not favourable. Robbie Williams is a huge star. You need look no further than his record-breaking deal with EMI to see how powerful and influential he has become. If he says a track is going on his album then who is going to argue with him. How many EMI executives would feel safe in their jobs if they put their heads above the parapet and offered the opinion that Rob should stick to playing the tune to his nearest and dearest at family parties and dump it from *Escapology*? One thing you can be pretty sure of is that if an unknown Robert Peter Williams was to turn up in the plush reception of EMI's London HQ, guitar in hand, offering to play the song to the top brass, you can guarantee security would have him out the door before you could say: 'Nutter in the lobby'.

April 1 2003 was D-day. The consensus within the Robbie Williams camp was that if *Escapology* did not break him in America, nothing would. Rob began the month with an exhausting round of PR to push the album. He was booked to appear on NBC's *Last Call* with Carson Daly at the Rockefeller Centre and he was lined up for an appearance on *Good Morning America*. The signs were good. The Stateside music critics were in the main giving the thumbs up to *Escapology*. This would be the record that added the final territory to Williams's global domination. They had, of course, said that about other Robbie Williams records. The problem, hitherto, had been that the record-buying public had, in the main, steadfastly ignored the opinions of the experts. His last pop album *Sing When You're Winning* had sold only 126,000 copies in America. There were also those who felt "Feel" would not dramatically change the situation. Jim Kaminski, a pop–rock buyer for Tower Records in New York, says: 'It is a very good pop song, but it may be too European for an American market.' Rob himself had put down his failure to dent the US charts to his Britishness, his colloquial style, his sense of humour. The truth was, and is, that few can understand or explain why it hasn't happened for him in America. *Escapology* would be Williams's calling card to the US. 'No British record has ever made such a naked lunge for the American market,' said Alexis Petridis in *The Guardian*. "Song 3", a reference to "Song 2", which broke Blur in the US, has Williams, shrieking like the brainwash victim of a cult: 'You gotta love LA! …God I love LA! … California Baby! … I dig LA! Gotta Love LA! California USA! USA! USA!' 'He could make no more brazen an appeal to America,' said Petridis, 'if he came on stage dressed as the Statue of Liberty, unfurled the Stars and Stripes, set fire to an effigy of Saddam Hussein, then launched into "Yankie Doodle Dandy". Williams does everything but get down on his knees and beg America to like him.'

Back home, Rob had won yet another Brit Award, as Best Male Artist. His tour planned for the summer was an instant sell-out. The sale of tickets for his gigs at Knebworth broke the record set by rivals Oasis after selling out two nights in under seven hours. More than a thousand of the £35 tickets were selling per minute as the phone lines were opened. The

121,000 allocations of tickets for the first of his August shows at the Hertfordshire venue were sold in 30 minutes. Europe-wide, 650,000 tickets, grossing more than £22 million, were sold in just one day.

EPILOGUE
pop idol

Like millions of others, Robbie Williams was gripped by the horror that was the television show *Popstars*. It was the car crash appeal of it: you know you should look away, but you just can't. There was something scarily compulsive about it, an obscene voyeurism that made you watch those poor deranged souls as they paraded their large egos and low self-esteem to a nation debased by the spectacle. Rob thought it was exploitation. He also reckons that if he had been one of the *Popstars* wannabes he would have never have made it into the band. He's kidding himself – he would have walked it.

The whole point of the second *Popstars* incarnation, *Pop Idol,* was to find the next Robbie Williams. Can you imagine boy-faced, sub-Donny Osmond warbler Gareth Gates up against Robbie in the final? It would have been halted to stop the stuttering song-wrecker from taking undue punishment. Williams is the ultimate pop star. There will be many more Gareths and Will Youngs out there who'll take a shot at the title, but they don't come close. Robbie was pure-bred for the role, that's his purpose, it's why he's there.

To his primary constituency of women, it is his many obvious human failings that have proved to be his most durable asset. Women want to save Williams, to rescue, nurture, cure him. They see his pain and a million years of conditioning kicks in. Females, whose previous Angel of Mercy skills had stretched to 'Shut it, you moaning git', all feel that they, and they alone, could make the troubled Robbie happy again. He elicits the budding mothering instinct in 12-year-olds and reawakens it in the HRT generation. Women feel no shame in loving Robbie. Yes, the attraction is physical – young women already bored with their pasty-faced Mr Right-ish want to sleep with him – but it is also about the primal desire to protect and heal. After the sex there would be some serious work to be done.

The feeling has not always been mutual. Williams seems, at best, to be ambivalent in his attitude to women. None has so far lived up to the standard set by his adored mother, Jan. His relationships with girlfriends have been notable for their brevity. His fling with Rachel Hunter burnt out early in 2003 amid claims that she could no longer deal with his moods and self-obsession. Explaining his failure to find the female partner, he insists he craves, Rob says: 'They seem to be too boring or too full of female intuition. All I want is someone I can talk to and have a laugh with and who happens to be incredible looking and a filthy little minx.' Witness, too, his less than gentlemanly approach to the fans he sleeps with on tour. In the film of his *Sermon on the Mount* tour, *Nobody Someday*, he caddishly brags about bedding the smitten girls then degrades them on screen. They become fodder for his gags, his anecdotes. He affects their foreign accents and denounces them as nutters from 'Planet Fan' or obsessives with the deranged notion that by sleeping with him they might be starting a relationship with him.

Likewise, the relationship with his fans seems to be a case of love–hate. He will openly complain about an audience: they were cold, lacking in energy, dead. He will stand on a stage in from of 10,000 or 15,000 of his European fans, with the demonic wide-eyed stare of the football thug and safely away from his microphone stand yell at them: 'Come on, you fucking bastards', while giving them a clench-fisted salute. The behaviour does nothing to discredit him in their eyes. There is an instant connection there, an understanding. Rob has laid himself so bare, so open to his public that his history infects everything he does. You cannot listen to a Robbie Williams song without your impression of the record being shaped by your knowledge of the singer. When he sings in "Come Undone" 'because I'm scum and I'm your son' he is talking to everyone, acknowledging his previous misdeeds and asking our forgiveness. He knows we are aware of the battles he has fought within himself; it is a shared history. We know he was the beaten puppy who came out of Take That scarred and wounded, conquered his many problems and emerged from them victorious. That's why his fans will forgive him his overblown ego, his self-indulgence and petulance. It is the Williams mantra that the British public will forgive you anything as long as you're good. When, in early 2003, Rob performed at the Rock the Vote gig in New York along with a host of other acts, he gave the usual accomplished Williams performance. The audience was polite, but patently unmoved. Perhaps, until the Americans can relate to him in the same way we do, his dream of becoming as a big a star in the US as here will remain just that.

At his lowest ebb, in the grip of a losing battle with alcohol and drugs, Rob decided he wanted to kill himself, to stop the pain, put an end to it. He had bought four grams of cocaine and had taken a huge dose of it before climbing on to a tenth-floor balcony with the intention of throwing himself off. Around the same time he made a depressing prediction. 'I think I'm going to die before I'm 30,' he said. 'I don't know why I've got this feeling that it will turn out like that. I have quite a strong sense about it. That's why I try to live each day as fully as I possibly can. That means hitting the clubs often drugged up to the eyeballs.' Thankfully Rob is still looking good for February 13, 2004, when he will reach the milestone he predicted would elude him. By the middle of 2003 he had been dry for two and a half years. His Beverly Hills home is alcohol-free. Nobody who enters the house is allowed to drink. Instead of clubs, Rob and his friends will go for a coffee. He has a chef to prepare him low-fat food. On the rare occasions he goes out for dinner, he will visit a small restaurant near his home for an early dinner around 5.30 p.m. and will usually be home two hours later. Guests at the house usually find little to do after 9.30. The one-time wild man, the archetypal party animal has gone. In his place is the new focused, clean-living Rob. Only two packs a day of Silk Cut remain of the cocktail of stimulants that once controlled him.

The insecurities and neuroses that have defined him remain too. The constant struggle between the larger-than-life character he created for public consumption and the real man looms large. Robbie was created, says Williams, because Robert would never have the guts to get up on stage. He continues to be troubled by his fame. On the one hand he rails at being such very public property, yet dreads a time when his star fades. He is also acutely aware of his image as a 'real person', someone his fans can relate to. He plays with the theme in his song "Handsome Man" on *Escapology*. 'Y'all know who I am, I'm still the boy next door. That's if you're Lord Lichfield and Roger Moore,' he sings. Yet, how in touch with real people can you be in your Hollywood hacienda? When Rob recorded the seemingly ego-crazed lyrics to "Handsome Man" he wanted to sing the lines 'Lonely, so lonely, God knows,' as a counterbalance to his outrageous bragging. It's a recurring theme. The richer and more successful you get, the more cut off you become from the real world. Rob is rarely alone. He is constantly surrounded by groups of corporate lackeys, hangers-on, gofers and minders. Increasingly, they have become like family to the star. These people love him and like him, he says optimistically. The problem for anyone in his position is fundamentally this: those people are there primarily because they are paid to be. It is not, when all is said and done, a relationship of equals. Rob is their boss and they are expected to do what he wants. It is a superstar's privilege to keep people waiting or stand them up, but it doesn't make them like you.

It is the same on tour. Rob will talk about the 'love I feel in this room' when he is surrounded by his band and crew. But music tours are notoriously incestuous and also back-biting. It is very difficult to have a friendship with somebody you work for. The bottom line is that Rob has the power over these people's livelihoods. He has the right to hire and fire. When all is said and done, few people actually like their bosses. It is a sad fact that you can't retain that level of control over somebody's life and expect them to enjoy it. Those who have witnessed at first hand the entourage surrounding the singer speak of the often sickening sycophancy at work. For the loveably 'real' Robbie it is an unreal world. How do you know your jokes are funny if your audience is paid to laugh?

Success has bought Rob a mansion in the most exclusive district of LA with stars like Tom Jones as neighbours, but he remains, by the standards of peers like Elton John, relatively frugal. When he was showing a TV crew round his Beverly Hills home for an episode of MTV *Cribs* he had to borrow a Bentley to make it look like he had amassed all the prerequisite rock star toys. In one seemingly outrageous piece of celebrity decadence he paid £250,000 for a platinum pool table. He actually bought it in a fit of pique when the New York shop assistant, not recognizing the British singer, told the scruffy-looking shopper he wouldn't be able to afford it.

As he approaches his 30th birthday, Rob reaches a crucial stage in his life both professionally and personally. He says he wants children, but shows no signs of finding a relationship that would fulfil his wish. He seems pathologically unable or unwilling to put the past to rest. Even after all these years and all his success, his bitterness remains. On a 'hidden' track on *Escapology* he revisits his feud with Gary Barlow and can't resist a jibe at his old enemy's expense. As an artist he has reached the height of his powers. Only success in America could add to his popularity. As always, there are those who question his ability to continue these levels of incredible success. There is a commonly held opinion in the music business that Rob's career can go no further. The perceived wisdom is that anybody who is likely to buy a Robbie Williams record has got one already. He can't improve on where he is. In the US, too, he faces many hurdles. He is up against fellow ex-boy band star Justin Timberlake, who is at 22 seven years his junior. Although only a year younger than Rob, fellow rival Enrique Inglesias has enjoyed success in the States for more than three years and has established a loyal fan base. Regardless of the challenges, few would bet against Williams.

At the German launch for *Escapology* Rob was forecasting a downward turn in his career prospects. 'I think after this tour and this album it's all downhill, I genuinely do,' he said. 'This is the pinnacle of my career right now, so come and see me in a holiday camp like Butlins in five years with Oasis.' Unlikely, yes, but what a show it would be!